"Even after years of experience, every preacher faces the same question every week: 'What will I say next Sunday?' These sermons from Richard Lischer, one of the finest teachers of preaching, demonstrate there is something more at work when the preacher approaches the pulpit than cranking out another message. There is the high drama between the congregation, the pastor, the context in which they live—and a holy word from God. Like all good teachers, here he is not explaining this drama but revealing it."

— M. Craig Barnes
president, Princeton Theological Seminary

...out humanity. Because ...od is. And the God he ...t discovered ourselves ...ut be careful. First ask

— Samuel Wells
author of *Walk Humbly: Encouragements for Living, Working, and Being*

"This wonderful collection from Richard Lischer reminds us why the sermon is the original and greatest theological genre. There is more packed in this book than in a whole passel of academic monographs—and in much more compelling prose. Press this book into the hands of your local preacher and say, 'More like these, please!'"

— Sarah Hinlicky Wilson
Tokyo Lutheran Church, Japan
Institute for Ecumenical Research, Strasbourg, France

"Compelled by the gospel of Jesus Christ, Richard Lischer tells the truth and nothing but the truth about suffering, hope, and courage for the living of these days. These sermons are from a trusted sage who will lead readers once again to meet and follow the incarnate Way of truth."

— Luke A. Powery
Duke Divinity School

Just Tell the Truth

A Call to Faith, Hope, and Courage

Richard Lischer

WILLIAM B. EERDMANS PUBLISHING COMPANY
GRAND RAPIDS, MICHIGAN

Wm. B. Eerdmans Publishing Co.
4035 Park East Court SE, Grand Rapids, Michigan 49546
www.eerdmans.com

27 26 25 24 23 22 21   1 2 3 4 5 6 7

ISBN 978-0-8028-7884-7

Library of Congress Cataloging-in-Publication Data

Names: Lischer, Richard, author.
Title: Just tell the truth : a call to faith, hope, and courage / Richard
    Lischer.
Other titles: Sermons. Selections.
Description: Grand Rapids, Michigan : William B. Eerdmans Publishing
    Company, [2021] | Includes bibliographical references. | Summary:
    "A collection of biblically and theologically rooted sermons about
    living the Christian life with conviction"—Provided by publisher.
Identifiers: LCCN 2020036704 | ISBN 9780802878847 (paperback)
Subjects: LCSH: Christian life—Sermons. | Sermons, American. |
    Evangelical Lutheran Church in America—Sermons. | Lutheran
    Church—Sermons.
Classification: LCC BV4501.3 .L566 2021 | DDC 252—dc23
LC record available at https://lccn.loc.gov/2020036704

For Tracy

Because of where we are
And where we've been

Wherever you turn your eyes the world can shine like transfiguration. You don't have to bring a thing to it except a little willingness to see. Only, who could have the courage to see it?

—REVEREND JOHN AMES IN *GILEAD*
BY MARILYNNE ROBINSON

CONTENTS

The Life of Faith

For All the Saints

Public Callings

INTRODUCTION

This collection originated in several ways. Most of the pieces were sermons preached in churches or chapels, the names of which I remember with pleasure and list at the end of this introduction. The sermons were accompanied by singing and prayers and in most cases followed by the movement of people toward the altar for communion. In other words, most of the messages in this collection were not isolated from the assembly of worshipers, the responses of attentive listeners, and the fidgeting and fussing of children. A few of the sermons I reformatted as essays for publication in books and journals. Others began as meditations—briefer, less developed commentary for smaller groups. Still others began as essays, then were reconceived as sermons and found their way into the oral-aural milieu of churches. For more than three decades my home base has been a divinity school, and therefore a few of the sermons have a student and faculty congregation in mind. The only criterion I observed in selecting these pieces was their echoing relevance to the Christian gospel and their usefulness to a new reading audience.

The sermons come with memories of the ministry from which they emerged and of the people in the pews (or on folding chairs) who with great patience did the hard work of engaging with the spoken word of God. Implicit in each chapter are the stories of confessions and conflicts, friendships, betrayals, and everyday love—most of them necessarily untold—because it's impossible to bring so many hidden dramas to the surface of a twenty-minute, public talk.

Some years ago the literary critic John Ciardi wrote an influential book called *How Does a Poem Mean?* It may be time to ask, "How does a sermon mean?" Especially sermons that are now cut loose from their original environment. The word "sermon" means conversation, but in their printed form the conversations have become quieter and more reflective.

The chapters of this book draw on three fields of meaning.

The first belongs to the preacher or author, who in the process of interpretation has developed an insight into the meaning of the text and a plan for getting it across. What do I think is most important about this text or occasion? In what ways will the message reflect the theme, mood, and style of its source in Scripture? How shall I translate the grace of God into grace-filled speech for others?

The second field of meaning (or maybe the first) belongs to the hearer. A hearer or reader harbors certain expectations—a need, a hope, a question, a way of looking at things—that he or she brings to the message. You might think of the sermon as a picnic to which the preacher brings the basket and the listener brings the sandwiches. When the need is great enough, we may even say the listener "makes" the sermon. If that's true, and, without overstating the case, I think it is, there will be a lot of sermons being preached in any given worship service!

In between the speaker's meaning and the listener's experience lies a vast and complex field that, for lack of a more original term, we may call the *context* of the message. It is social, political, communal, and cultural. It is "the way things are" at any given moment. No one communicates from some airless, context-free environment, because there is no such thing, and we should never pretend there is. Those who try to preach (or write) in a timeless manner are doomed to reach no one in particular. This middle field provides a frame, or cultural theater, in which the message and the hearer's understanding of it interact.

"Only connect," E. M. Forster said about writing. Sorting through the fields of meaning may be the most difficult thing about preaching or writing. The hermeneutical gyroscope is always spinning—at a hospital, at a ball game, in bedtime reading, at lunch with friends— the work never lets you alone. As the fictional preacher John Ames says in Marilynne Robinson's *Gilead*, "When you do this sort of work, it seems to be Sunday all the time, or Saturday night. You just finish preparing for one week and its already the next week."

In selecting these messages, two contexts stood out to me. The first is sociopolitical. I am referring to the growing disregard for any standard of truth that permeates our social discourse. The climate of free-for-all falsity is everywhere, both in politics and in media: language without foul lines, which is like baseball without an umpire. The dribble of misinformation we have grudgingly learned to tolerate has morphed into something like a raging virus that corrupts everyone and everything it touches. It breeds cynicism and distrust at all levels. Even if you don't believe the lies, it's hard not to be exhausted and depressed by them. One hundred years ago William Butler Yeats wrote *the* poem of the twentieth century, "The Second Coming." He might have been describing the empty talk of our age: "The best lack all conviction, while the worst / Are full of passionate intensity." That sentence alone is enough to place Yeats among the prophets.

The title of this book, *Just Tell the Truth*, does not refer to politics, science, history, or media. Of course, politicians, scientists, historians, and pundits must tell the truth according to the standards of their respective professions. And so must Christians. For us, telling the truth begins with an accurate and passionate account of what the book of Acts calls "the facts about Jesus"—who he is, what he did, what he demands, and the sort of people he empowers us to be. I can't think of a more modest proposal than the one I am making: that Christians of all parties and in all walks of life simply tell the truth about what it really means to be a follower of the Way.

The second field of meaning came late, as I was in the final stages of preparing the manuscript. COVID-19 created a universal field of suffering and anxiety to such an extent that it was impossible to think or write about anything else. As I write, it is everyone's context. While some are hunkered down and learning to appreciate the simpler existence that COVID requires, others are being ruined by it, many losing their livelihoods, others their very lives.

Several of the late sermons in this volume reflect the terrible context of the novel coronavirus and the new meaning it has imposed on our collective existence. Two chapters in particular, a meditation for

Holy Saturday and a sermon preached in an empty church, address the pandemic directly. Preparing a manuscript a full year in advance of its publication, during a time in which the death toll in some cities is doubling every three days, is nothing short of an act of faith on the part of my publisher and my editor. For me personally, writing in a time of plague makes of this book a prayer. "Save your people and bless your inheritance; be their shepherd and carry them forever." Unavoidably, I now read the section "Waiting in Hope" through a very different lens. I believe you will too.

I am grateful to two former students and now colleagues in ministry, Dr. Jennifer Copeland and Rev. Andrew Jacob Tucker, who, several years apart, offered to sift through and edit decades-worth of my sermons. Though flattered by their offers, I stalled, knowing that the necessary editing couldn't be done by anyone but me and the reward would never repay the tremendous effort they were willing to give. So, impulsively, I plowed through them myself and became my own editor, arranger, and worst critic. But it's doubtful I would have done any of it were it not for their suggestions and enthusiasm. In addition, I owe perennial thanks to John F. Thornton of the Spieler Agency in New York City, whose critical advice, experience, and friendship have supported me over the years.

This book, like several others, is dedicated to my wife Tracy for reasons that really don't belong in the introduction to a book.

Scriptural quotations in this book are not limited to one translation of the Bible. More often than not, I follow the New Revised Standard Version, but in some of the sermons I draw instinctively from translations that are more beautiful, more accurate, or more precious to me, usually the Revised Standard Version or the King James Version of the Bible.

With gratitude to the following congregations in which these sermons were preached:

Prince of Peace Lutheran Church, Virginia Beach, Virginia
Duke University Chapel, Durham, North Carolina

York Chapel, Duke Divinity School
Goodson Chapel, Duke Divinity School
St. Paul's Lutheran Church, Durham, North Carolina
Grace Lutheran Church, Durham, North Carolina
Memorial Church, Harvard University, Cambridge,
   Massachusetts
Second Presbyterian Church, Roanoke, Virginia
First Presbyterian Church, Durham, North Carolina
Trinity Church, Boston, Massachusetts
The Gathering Church, Durham, North Carolina
Mary and Martha Lutheran Church, Durham, North
   Carolina
Grace Lutheran Church, River Forest, Illinois
Lake Junaluska Conference and Retreat Center, Lake Ju-
   naluska, North Carolina
Montreat Conference Center, Montreat, North Carolina
First United Methodist Church, Birmingham, Michigan
Holden Village, Chelan, Washington
United Metropolitan Missionary Baptist Church, Winston-
   Salem, North Carolina
First Baptist Church, Asheville, North Carolina

Richard Lischer
Easter 2020

A Season of Suffering

I

The Shape of Ashes

"Remember, you are dust, and unto dust you will return."
—GENESIS 3:19B,
BOOK OF COMMON PRAYER

Among Christians, marking with ashes first occurred in the early Middle Ages as a sign of sorrow and repentance. Perhaps if you had lived then, with the Visigoths and the bubonic plague bearing down on you, when the slogan of the day was *memento mori* ("remember, you will die") and a woman's average life expectancy was thirty-two years, you too would have thought it was a splendid idea to show up at church once a year in sackcloth and ashes.

The symbol of ashes emerges from the depths of the earth. It is as old as fire, as bitter as shame, and as fundamental as death. When Abraham decides to bargain with God over the destruction of Sodom and Gomorrah, he says to God, "Who am I to bargain with you? I am nothing but dust and ashes." After King David's daughter, Tamar, is raped by her own brother, the Scripture says she covered her head with ashes. The ash heap is where we find Job, scraping the sores on his body with a piece of broken pottery.

On Ash Wednesday, as the sun was coming up, a young woman stood outside a Starbucks with a bowl of ashes and a word for those about to begin their morning commute. She offered nothing more than the sign of the cross and this reminder: "Remember, you are dust, and unto dust you will return." I'm told the line of those waiting for this blessing was very long.

If you have ever carried the ashes of a fellow human being in one of those bronze boxes provided by the mortuary, you must admit that your first thought is not of repentance or shame or even God, but only of mortality. You ask yourself, how has this beloved human, with whom I once shared laughter and tears, become nothing more than humus, the stuff of the earth?

Of course, if you love the earth, you tell yourself that this is all natural and good. In her novel *A Thousand Acres*, Jane Smiley writes of the goodness of her farmland: "For millennia, water lay over the land. Untold generations of water plants, birds, animals, insects lived, shed bits of themselves, and died. . . . It all drifted down, lazily, in the warm, soupy water—leaves, seeds, feathers, scales, flesh, bones, petals, pollen—then mixed with the saturated soil below and became, itself, soil. They were the soil, and the soil was the treasure."

But before you can say that the process of "earth to earth, ashes to ashes" is good, you have to believe it's going to happen not to the other guy but to you. Many of the men and women I work with belong to the demographic known as "the Invincibles," the twenty-somethings who are declining health insurance on a massive scale because they are never going to get sick and, consequently, are never going to die.

The Invincibles are represented in our airport terminal by an enormous advertisement for a spa and fitness center. It features a buff young guy in a towel, still glistening from the morning workout. It reads, *"The human battery—infinitely rechargeable."* When you see it, you have to resist the urge to deface public property. Why? Because it's a *lie*! The human battery is *not* infinitely rechargeable. Who will tell us the truth about ourselves? What fashion line or pharmaceutical rep will admit that his or her product does not come with the guarantee of eternal life? Who will tell us the truth, a truth that is available in any church (and, at least, at one Starbucks) on any Ash Wednesday? You are dust and unto dust you will return?

The point of Ash Wednesday is not to rub everyone's nose in their own mortality. That would make us angels of death and not messengers of life. But we do have to make our way from the weight of ashes in that little box to what Saint Paul calls the weight of glory, which is in the resurrection of Jesus from the dead. And there *is* a way from one to the other.

The first station on the way from death to life is the "little death" of repentance. Repentance is the honest self-assessment, "I am nothing but dust and ashes." But these ashes are not merely symbols of my finite nature or physical limitations. They represent the many ways I have turned away from the love of God and pursued my own interests. Picturesquely, Luther said we are *incurvatus in se*, curved in upon ourselves. By that he did not mean *thoughtful* or *reflective* but self-obsessed. It's not a pretty metaphor. Our love is like a boomerang that, no matter how piously we aim it at others, always comes wheeling back to our own desires. The ashes stand for repentance.

Sometimes we mistake regret for repentance. It's been said that regret is an old man's disease, but what a shame it is to waste a perfectly good sin on the elderly. Anyone can wallow in regret; as Emily Dickinson says, "Remorse is memory awake." It's the disease, she says, that "Not even God can heal." Unlike remorse, repentance entails a turning away from yourself (including your regrets) toward someone who has the authority to give the definitive answer to your entire life. With regret, you are beating up on yourself and loving it. Repentance acknowledges the possibility of an answer that makes things right.

Repentance carries us toward the goal of reconciliation. The ultimate goal of Lent is not contrition or meditation on suffering but reconciliation. Paul explains to the Ephesians that Jesus came in order to "create in himself one new humanity in place of the two, thus making peace, and might reconcile both groups to God in one body through the cross."

A heart turned to God is prepared to turn toward others. Then, it is possible to forgive another human being—someone who has failed you, hated you, or betrayed you. It is possible, at least, to make something right with that person. You may not continue in close communion, but the sheer *fact* of what God has done means that a terrible breach has been repaired. Historically, the climax of Lent occurred in the first Mass of Maundy Thursday, when penitents came before the altar in sackcloth and ashes and were reconciled to the community. Then, as now, it took place beneath the all-important cross.

When I was an intern during my seminary days, I served in a large church where the minister performed about forty funerals a year. One morning he called me into his office and told me to take a funeral for him that afternoon. This made me uneasy. Apparently, I had skipped the class in which we learned how to bury people. I told him I didn't know how.

He sighed and walked me over to the parish hall, where he took a piece of chalk and, like a coach drawing up a three-point play, drew the outline of an imaginary grave on the linoleum floor. He told me where to stand, how to act, and what to say. Then he took a mysterious vial from his inside pocket and said, "These are the ashes. When you come to the committal, pour these at the head of the casket and say, 'Earth to earth, ashes to ashes, dust to dust.' And one more thing: don't be sloppy. Make sure you make the sign of the cross with the ashes."

I might have asked, "Why not be sloppy with the ashes? That's what death is all about, isn't it? A chaotic reunion with the soil, which itself is a chaos of commingled organisms on a planet named Earth."

But in Christ, even the chaos of ashes finds a form. We don't receive the ashes on Ash Wednesday only; we bring them to the altar every day. The little box we carry is our own. Only in Jesus are they gathered into the shape of the cross. Time and again, we bring our dust and ashes to him until there is nothing left of us and all that remains is the new thing that has been forming in us.

I can still hear my old mentor as he pulled the vial out of his coat. "Here are the ashes. Remember, the shape—the *shape*—is essential. Don't be sloppy."

2

The Gospel of Setting

And the Spirit immediately drove him out into the wilderness. He was in the wilderness forty days, tempted by Satan; and he was with the wild beasts; and the angels waited on him.

—MARK 1:12–13

If we even *think* about temptation these days, which is doubtful, it usually concerns someone torn between an absolute good and an absolute desire. The drama is half the fun. One thinks of young Joseph in the Old Testament standing in the bedroom of Potiphar's wife, she beckoning him toward the adulterous couch, he momentarily transfixed. Then, in an instant of moral and religious triumph, he flees the room. Nowadays, even the godliest of audiences to that scene feels a twinge of disappointment. In the perceived absence of absolutes, the very concept of temptation seems passé.

Or one thinks of Augustine's agony recorded in the *Confessions* over a few pears stolen as a teenager. It bothers Augustine that he had given in to temptation. It bothers Augustine that he doesn't even like pears.

We read Matthew's and Luke's accounts of the temptation, and we get the high drama and human desire we were looking for. There, the combatants taunt each other like Homeric warriors. There, we witness a titanic clash of personalities, with the victory going to the Word of God.

In Mark's Gospel it's quite different. There, the temptation is not a saga but a setting. There's no dialogue, no plot, not a hint of psychology, no human needs such as hunger, no clash of powers, and, worst of all, no recorded outcome. Jesus meets Satan in the wilderness for a cosmic battle, and Mark neglects to tell us who won. The only clue to its importance lies in the setting of this nonstory.

When our children were young, we loved those wilderness movies that recounted an urban family's hilarious adventures in the wilds of Colorado or Montana. We embraced an attitude that is shared by most urban and suburbanized folk—city bad, wilderness good. The wilderness being a wholesome place populated by cute chipmunks and friendly bear cubs. To people who are fed up with traffic, afraid of crime, sick with smog, Jesus's forty-day retreat looks inviting.

In the Bible, however, temptation is not a brief adventure but a way of life with a history all its own. It originated in another kind of wilderness, usually called a garden. There, humankind was alone except for the beasts. There was a tempter, a temptation to be something they were not created to be, a catastrophic failure, and finally angels with flaming swords. Later in the history of temptation, Israel passes through the waters of the Red Sea and gets lost in the wilderness for forty years. In the Old Testament the wilderness is not a place of wholesomeness but of apostasy. It was in the wilderness that Israel began to long for the fleshpots of Egypt. It was in the wilderness that Israel learned to say, "This manna stinks. Let's build a golden calf."

Later in this history, another son of God walks into the river to be baptized. He too endures forty days of testing in the wilderness, where his companions are not Disney chipmunks but scorpions, jackals, wild boar, vultures circling endlessly by day, hyenas laughing uproariously by night—and of course, the angels. He will not see angels again until tested in another garden.

The Old Testament calls the wilderness *Jeshimon*, or "the devastation." According to one commentator, the wilderness is "an area of contorted strata, where the ridges run in all directions as if they were warped and twisted . . . the limestone is blistered and peeling; the rocks are bare and jagged . . . it glows and shimmers with heat like some vast furnace."

In the final act, we are the players in this drama. In the mirror of this story, we too become sons and daughters in the water, and in our most lucid moments we recognize our cultural environment for the "contorted," "twisted" wasteland it is. In times of testing we pray, "O God, you know the deep places through which our lives must pass. Be with us when we enter them, and by the ministry of your angels and the power of your Son, deliver us."

I once had a mentor who, every time we met, would ask, "How goes the battle?" I never asked but often wondered, "What battle are you talking about?" I think I get it now. It's possible to level off the Christian life and to round off its edges to the extent that we miss its *eventfulness*. History is not without its crises; why should the Christian life be? It shouldn't be treated as a series of lifestyle choices but as the life-or-death struggle it is. It was necessary for the Spirit to *drive* Jesus into the wilderness. Who would choose to go there?

Writing to a friend in 1956, the writer Flannery O'Connor, who was to die of lupus at thirty-nine, recognizes her particular setting for the proving ground that it is: "I have never been anywhere but sick. In a sense sickness is a place, more instructive than a long trip to Europe, and it's always a place where there's no company, where nobody can follow. Sickness before death is a very appropriate thing and I think those who don't have it miss one of God's mercies."

In the 1960s, when black churches were being firebombed with regularity, it was not uncommon for Martin Luther King and his associates to rush to the scene of a bombing and conduct a service in the ashes of the gutted sanctuary. I have spoken to people who were present on such occasions. I would ask, "What did he say?" They would respond, "I don't remember." Then they would add, "But I will never forget *where* he said it." It was enough that someone had taken the gospel into the devastation and proclaimed its authority over every power threatening to destroy it.

At a church reunion, a married couple says, "We remember your ministry to us." "Really?" comes the reply along with an undisguisable blank look. "It was in that little alcove outside the ER. It must have been midnight. Remember?" "Oh, yes. Of course."

Apparently, the gospel had found its proper location.

The nonstory of the temptation of Jesus in the wilderness is such a setting. For Mark, it's enough to say God was there. In his gospel, the temptation sets the stage for future tests. Demons will shriek at Jesus, Pharisees will snarl. Even his friends will desert him. The first unambiguous confession of faith will occur at the crucifixion when a Roman policeman will gesture toward a corpse on a cross and proclaim, "Surely, this was the Son of God."

If you are wondering where in the world is God, you needn't always look for the most dramatic or uplifting story. Look at the setting. See where he struggled. Consider where you struggle—with what addiction or anxiety, in what devastating circumstances.

The scene of domestic violence can become such a lonely and frightening setting. Who knows about it, or cares?

In a little town in Ohio, with the first opioid death in the community, the whole landscape changes, and Anytown, USA, becomes a wilderness of horrific testing.

One person eats some infected meat, and the entire world shudders to a halt. It's a battle.

At Golgotha Jesus wrestles again with his own demons. Once again, the Holy One of God is tested and convulsed. At the cross he experiences all the terrors that are. Only the one who has entered the Devastation can help you and me survive it.

If you want to know who won this cosmic battle, you are going to have to cheat a little and peek at the end of the book. In the meantime, it's enough to know, in the words of the hymn, "He's by our side upon the plain." The wilderness is still the wilderness. It's still the setting where there is little company and no one can follow. It's our territory.

But God is there.

3

Altar or Table?

He entered once for all into the Holy Place, not with the
blood of goats and calves, but with his own blood, thus
obtaining eternal redemption.

—HEBREWS 9:12

He was the word that spake it.
He took the bread and brake it;
and what that word did make it
I do believe and take it.

This simple sixteenth-century poem sums up the trust each of us
has as we prepare to receive the Lord's Supper. We believe and we
receive. It sounds simple, doesn't it? But we know that the contro-
versies regarding this sacrament have made it anything but simple.
What the church optimistically named the sacrament of unity has
often proved to be an occasion of disunity, setting off great argu-
ments among Christians over the status and makeup of its ordinary
elements. How can a modest piece of bread *be* the body of Christ?
What is the best way to receive the wine? Must there *be* wine?

These divisions have even extended to the piece of furniture on
which the elements are placed. What is it? Is it an altar or a table?
And does it matter? Or is it like the controversy raging throughout
Great Britain these days: not over Brexit—but tea. Does one first
pour milk in the cup and then add the tea, or tea first and then the

milk? Each has its advocates. More seriously, when the people of God eat their sacred meal, do they gather around a slaughter stone or a kitchen table? Does the symbolism matter?

A congregation I served had just begun to plan for a new sanctuary when it was forced to deal with this very question. The Methodist architect put it to us: tell me about your theology of the sacrament. What'll it be: an altar or a table? At the end of many earnest meetings and months of study, we made our weasel-worded reply. Make it a table, but a *very* substantial one.

Our instincts told us that there is something big and powerful looming behind the table, but we were unwilling to name it or let it go. What's behind the table? As an experiment, perhaps when you are sitting at table, ask a child this question: "Where does that slice of bread on your sandwich come from?"

"From this package."

"No, where, really?"

"Well, from the Kroger, I guess."

"No, silly, I mean where does it *come* from?"

When pressed, the child will admit that she thinks the bread comes from a truck. If you probe any deeper, you come to what archaeologists term "the inaccessibility of origins." And what is true of bread is also true of electricity, hamburgers, lunch money, good books, and iPods. Things just are. We are given our world.

To see how removed we are from the origins of things, wander through the streets of a Guatemalan village until, toward dusk, you hear an unearthly scream. A child in pain? A dog in heat? A murder in progress? Well, sort of. On the back stoop of a modest house a woman is calmly wringing a chicken's neck. It's supper time. She is preparing a meal that, from its source in the backyard, will be table-ready in a matter of hours. Compare her grandchildren, who are standing in the doorway nonchalantly watching the slaughter, with our grandchildren, who think that chicken comes from a kindly man with a white goatee, and one arrives at a truth about our culture.

Our culture shields us from origins, for often at the source of a commodity there is profound misery. Adults know this, children do not. So, children ask innocently, "Why do some Native Americans live on reservations?" "Why is Japan our special friend?" "Why are poor people poor?" "What are reparations?" Does one appreciate the product more if one understands the toil and pain that lay behind it? Would we enjoy our barbeque or fried chicken more if we could see the life of the hog or chicken in a North Carolina factory farm, to say nothing of the workers there? You can stroll into your favorite department store and buy a genuine suede jacket for $37. When you get it home, you will notice that it was made in Bangladesh, which is to say, somebody practically died to make your jacket. You are not alone if you would rather not think about it.

Most churches are shying away from the altar as a monolithic place of sacrifice in favor of a table.

At table there is harmony, unity, and good etiquette. The only sounds are those of ordinary conversation and the clink of sterling on china, or at least plastic on Styrofoam.

At the altar there is the braying and screeching of beasts being slaughtered. It's not conversation one hears, but a cry of dereliction. "My God, my God . . ."

At table there is the coziness of family relationships. One belongs at the table. Only for the most heinous of crimes is the child sent from the family table. There, at table the child has direct access to the parent.

At the altar is the alien and austere presence of the priest, the intermediary, who is neither father nor friend. One approaches the altar as one treads on holy ground, with fear and trembling.

At table there is bread, wine, and hospitality.

At the altar there is body, blood, carnage, and death.

Maybe you, like me, grew up at a good table. Okay, it was aluminum with a Formica top, but the people at the table were good. There was always a pot roast with carrots and potatoes or, to appease some ancestral god, German sauerkraut and spareribs, but the food was hot, and you could be yourself at the table and belong to something bigger than yourself at the same time. You could put up with comments like "Get your elbows off the table," because you were allowed to *be* at the table.

But if you are the kid I was, maybe you didn't appreciate all that made that table possible: A woman was holding down a low-paying job and doing her chores late into the night. A man was working one job Monday to Friday and another, more hateful job on Saturdays. Together they were spending their savings on medical care for parents and on the distant hope of a college education for their kid. If we fought, we tried not to do it at the table. It's a place of such intimacy that it almost invites betrayals. Who is the one who betrays me? "It's the one to whom I give this bread after I have dipped it into the dish we've been sharing. 'Take, eat.'"

The early Christians were sometimes accused of having no altar because they had done away with animal sacrifice. They were table people. They were accused of being atheists. Later in the letter, the writer of Hebrews asserts defiantly, "We *have* an altar from which those who serve in the Tabernacle have no right to eat." We have an altar. We consider Christ's entire act of self-sacrifice to be our altar. It is his cross, as stark and ugly and public as it can be, that makes our little table possible. So, maybe we don't have the ideal dinner hour or the perfect family to enjoy it. Who does? But because of Jesus's sacrifice, we do have a family in which we can be ourselves and belong to something greater than ourselves.

Last month the university where I teach sponsored a discussion of the most divisive issue on campus—race. A few people, including the university president, gathered around a table that looked for all the world like my old table—aluminum, Formica—on a set that reproduced an old-timey kitchen. It wasn't just a feel-good session, however, because everyone agreed that a lot of suffering had gone into making that table possible. We remembered the pioneering black students who, despite their official acceptance, faced exclusion every day. We remembered how Dr. King claimed to see white people and black people seated at the "table of brotherhood," which was only possible because of the blood and suffering of many. We can break bread today because behind our table looms the outline of something more substantial. As Maya Angelou says, "You have been paid for at a distant place."

And yet for all its horror and carnage, the altar can be a place of refuge. For it symbolizes the method of God's own sacrifice. "For when Christ came as a high priest . . . he entered once for all into the Holy Place, not with the blood of goats and calves, but with his own blood, thus obtaining eternal redemption." In the novel *Slaughterhouse Five* by Kurt Vonnegut, a group of Allied soldiers is captured and herded into a defunct meatpacking plant near Dresden. It is a slaughterhouse in which they will be incarcerated. How the prisoners hate the dank basement of that place! But when the firebombing of Dresden begins, the slaughterhouse no longer seems cold and inhospitable. Slaughterhouse No. 5 becomes a place of refuge.

On Maundy Thursday, while sitting at table, Jesus considered himself a dead man and spoke of a body broken, blood poured out, and other subjects not usually mentioned at table. Clearly, the slaughter stone was on his mind. He said, in effect, "This meal will not be free. All the forgiveness and love in this little room are going to cost Somebody something terrible."

Then, with his typical generosity, he snapped his fingers and said, "Check, please."

4

NIGHT

*So, after receiving the piece of bread, he immediately went
out. And it was night.*

—JOHN 13:21–30

Is it just me, or do you too feel a certain sympathy for this man Judas?
I would like to hear his side of the story, but he has no lines in this
episode or anywhere in the Gospel of John. You want to hear him ask
the Director, "What's my motivation in this scene?" And you would
give anything to hear the Director's reply. But there will be no solilo-
quy revealing the hidden motives or the human side of Judas. In the
Gospel of Matthew, the last we see of him is his bloated corpse twist-
ing beneath a sycamore tree. In the Gospel of John it is more terrible.
At supper the Lord dips the bread in the mixture of apples, walnuts,
wine, and honey—the *charoset*—and gives it to his disciple. Judas
receives the morsel, no doubt studying at it as if it were a message with
his name on it, which in a way it was, and darts from the room.

The gospel adds, "And it was night."

The night has become a character in the play, like a toxic cloud
trying to force its way into a room filled with warmth and love. Judas
closes the door on friends, fellowship, and feast, and walks out into
the darkness. And the night receives him as one of its own. He has
become a living commentary on the narrator's prophecy: "And this
is the judgment, that the light has come into the world, and people
loved darkness rather than light."

It has always been taken for granted that Judas got what he deserved. His end is terrible because what he did was terrible. The night is out there waiting for anyone who betrays the Lord. It's one thing to do what you have to do, but quite another to betray love. Love has no way of defending itself. No pain can compare with the betrayal of love. And to do it at *table*, where every day we renew both our bodies and our relationships with one another, only magnifies the crime.

Perhaps we are not capable of imagining a betrayal at supper. We take the drive-through lane, relay our order electronically to our unseen host, throw it into second gear, and we're gone. There's not enough time for a betrayal. If we're home, a betrayal of friendship occurring over TV trays and Szechuan takeout is hard to imagine. Serious conversation will only distract from the movie or ball game we are watching. The meal itself *is* a betrayal of other values.

But if you are reclining in Jewish fashion at a five-course feast of lamb and bread, greens, and the fruit of the vine, and if that meal is an expression of the family's very identity, a betrayal shatters everything the table stands for. The meal is a haven, one that Judas first violates and then forsakes.

Yet I do feel for him, this Judas, because, like you, I understand that anyone can be lost, not because they've made a mistake but because they are tragically caught in something larger than themselves. There are clues in this story and in this gospel. The Fourth Gospel is unique in its portrayal of Jesus, who is always in control of his own destiny. Only in John does Jesus say of his disciples, "I know whom I have chosen." Only in John does Jesus rule the world from the cross. In this gospel the soldiers come with their pathetic torches and lanterns, asking, "Are you Jesus of Nazareth?" And when he replies, "I am," it is the voice of the great I AM, and the soldiers fall back in a heap. No one tricks, traps, or betrays such a figure, any more than one captures a magnificent animal with a cheap net. No, this episode has been planned for some time, and from headquarters.

In "The Convergence of the Twain," Thomas Hardy imagines another sort of inevitability, the collision of the *Titanic* with an iceberg:

And as the smart ship grew
In stature, grace and hue,
In shadowy silent distance grew the iceberg too;
Till the Spinner of the Years
Said "Now!" And each one hears,
And consummation comes, and jars two hemispheres.

If it was *necessary*, as the Scripture says, that the Son of Man should suffer and die, what does that make Judas? Actor or pawn? During Holy Week we hear the Spinner of the Years say, "Now!" Judas's action is mysteriously contained within the freedom of the God who says, "I kill and I make alive; I wound and I heal; and no one can deliver out of my hand."

Instead of recognizing the terrible part assigned to Judas, we have focused on his evil and magnified it one hundredfold. The early church whispered legends about Judas to the effect that his body was so filled with immorality that it exploded and was eaten by maggots. In *The Divine Comedy* Dante places him in the center of hell, packed in ice, chewed eternally by Satan. "Judas" is like "Hitler," a name that contains the evil of countless anonymous people, just as the word "cancer" carries overtones of decay in many, nonmedical forms.

I feel sympathy for Judas because he and I are related. We need him to explain our own betrayals. He is our scapegoat. We project onto Judas all our infidelities and send him out into the night while we remain at our Lord's breast. But who is the betrayer here?

Who is it who blamed (and continues to blame) "the Jews" for the death of Jesus and made them scapegoats for our every ill? Whose missionaries helped take this land from its inhabitants and subjugated them in the name of Jesus? Who was it who cherry-picked some Bible passages in support of slavery and segregation? Who was it who erased the women from the sacred story and denied them leadership in Christ's church? Who is it who fails to welcome the sojourner and the immigrant and thereby closes doors that God wants opened? Who is it who bandies around the name "Christian" and cynically uses it for political advantage? Who? When the Soviet Union executed a traitor, the victim's family was forced to buy the ammunition, the idea being that even the best of families is responsible for its worst member. Maybe it's time for the church to pay up for brother Judas.

Despite the Bible's talk about Judas's greed, betrayal does not begin with money. It begins in pride. Take Simon Peter, another actor in this terrible night. We meet him as he warms himself by the light of a charcoal fire in the high priest's courtyard. He is given an opportunity to make the good confession but instead can only say, "I don't know the man." His betrayal is more than an impulsive lapse. It is a sequel to an earlier betrayal, when he promised that he would never make such a mistake. "I will never betray you." He spoke as if he, Simon Peter, had the moral capacity to be faithful to the Lord, as if faith in Jesus *is* a moral capacity. Even poor Judas admits to being acquainted with Jesus (which is better than Peter). In his own perverse way, Judas leads others to Jesus.

The story of Judas and Jesus tells us something about ourselves we would rather not face. The mystery of evil does not reside *out there* in the night. Betrayal comes from within the circle of love. The family is its incubator. Our university held a storytelling competition for eighteen-year-old freshmen—bright, accomplished, many from the "best families." They were invited to select one topic and speak on it. Their choice of subject? Betrayal.

In his famous memoir *Night*, Elie Wiesel remembers how he and his father were routed through German concentration camps. His father was growing weaker and had become a burden to his teenaged son. The boy thought, "If only I could get rid of this dead weight. Immediately," Wiesel adds, "I felt ashamed of myself, ashamed forever." One night, as he lay in the top bunk, he listened but did not intervene while the guards beat his father to death. Later a guard said to him, "Here there are no fathers, no brothers, no friends. Everyone lives and dies for himself alone."

All the world's betrayals are cradled in the story of Judas's betrayal of Jesus. We should not call him Judas; we should call him Everyman. If there is any miracle, it is that after all these years and despite our many advances, we still recognize ourselves in this story and are capable of being moved by it. Even on our best days, we are creatures of the night, or at least the twilight. We (and the institutions that protect us) are swathed in shadows and unsavory histories.

For too long we've assumed that the key to understanding the events of Holy Week is answering the question, who killed Jesus? Was it a Jewish sword or a Roman bullet? Was it a doomed Judas or a cowardly Simon Peter or a spineless Pontius Pilate? It doesn't matter. We are all a part of what the preacher Carlisle Marney called the "company of betrayers," for whom Jesus placed himself in the betrayable position. He had to be betrayed for *our* sins and not just those of our little brother.

Later in this gospel Jesus will encounter Peter at another charcoal fire. It's no longer night but daybreak on the beach. He's grilling some fresh-caught fish for his disciples, including Peter the Denier. I think he would have cooked for Judas too. He doesn't rehearse the events that belonged to the night. He doesn't reprise or rebuke the darkness. What he says to Peter he says to us as well, "Do you love me? Feed my sheep."

We have not barricaded the night from this church, for that would barricade Jesus too. He seeks out the night in all of us. That's where he wants to meet us, where things are darkest and where love has faltered. That's where his love is most effective. Tonight, the meal we celebrate is more than a memorial to one man's act of betrayal. It is a redemptive meal "given and shed for your sins." Our trust is this, that when the Lord hands us this morsel along with the cup of wine, he will have as sweet a word for us as he did for our brother Judas:

"Friend."

5

STRIPPED BARE

Jesus, knowing that the Father had given all things into his hands, . . . rose from supper, laid aside his garments, and girded himself with a towel.

—JOHN 13:3–4

At an appropriate time, the altar is stripped and, if possible, the crosses are removed from the church. It is expedient that any crosses that remain in the church be veiled.

ROMAN MISSAL

Undressing another person, or another person's body, is slow and ex- quisite work. Whether it's a feeble parent who can't manage the but- tons, a child for a bath, or an expectant lover, undressing can be an act of love. When a Jew dies, a small group known as *chevra kadisha* prepares the body for burial. First the body is reverently undressed, and any wounds on it are carefully cleansed. Rings, bracelets, and all jewelry are removed. The body is bathed and purified by water, then wrapped in a white sheet and perhaps a prayer cloth and tied with a sash secured by a sacred symbol. Now it is ready to meet the living God.

Each Maundy Thursday, the members of our church's altar guild carefully and lovingly remove the candelabra, cross, vessels, fine lin- ens, and paraments from the altar. They strip the altar to bare stone. When everything is removed, what is left is nude and vulnerable, not as imposing as one might expect. It seems almost a shame to see the al-

tar that way, and so when the women are finished undressing it, someone turns out the lights, and the congregation files out in silence.

Every time I participate in such a service, I think of Jesus, who on the
night of his betrayal laid aside his woven tunic and tied a towel around
his waist. He stripped for service. Another gospel tells us that later "they
stripped him" for mockery and death. The altar stands for Jesus, who in
Holy Week enters the last stages of his ritual purification.

The altar also stands for those from whom something or someone
is being taken away. It stands for us. A sentence from one of Dietrich
Bonhoeffer's prison letters comes to mind: "I think that even in this
place we ought to live as if we had no wishes and no future, and just
be our true selves." As a graduate student I read *Letters and Papers
from Prison* for the usual 1970s reasons, as an exhibit in the battle
between orthodoxy and what was then called secular theology. But
now I read it as an end-of-life narrative. I read it as the story of a
brilliant young man in a concentration camp who is preparing for his
own death, but not without a Gethsemane-like struggle.

In the spring of 1943 Bonhoeffer wrote to his friend Eberhard
Bethge, "I sometimes feel as if my life were more or less over. . . . But
you know, when I feel like this, there comes over me a longing (unlike
any other that I experience) to have a child and not to vanish without
a trace." By January 1945, he had adopted a fully retrospective view of
his own life. He made the telltale gesture of instructing his parents
to give away all his clothes, including the salt-and-pepper suit and
the pair of brown shoes. According to the witness of another prisoner, before he went to the gallows Bonhoeffer removed his prison
clothes and knelt in prayer. On April 9, 1945, the stripping of his
altar was complete.

When I was a child, it was the mysterious shadows that attracted
me to Holy Week. Nowadays it's something more, or something different. It's what draws me back to Bonhoeffer's *Letters* year after year.
In a church that's filled with people who are being reduced in a hundred different ways—by illness, death, grief, betrayal, depression, and
economic reversal, whose insurance has lapsed and whose dreams
have been foreclosed—Holy Week teaches us all a lesson in losing.

We are not losers, but we have been reduced, some of us to what feels like our touchstone. On Maundy Thursday we discover that even when everything has been taken away, something remains.

My South African friend Peter Storey once remarked that "America is the only country where more Christians go to church on Mother's Day than Good Friday." It's a sobering thought. The message of Easter, as the theologian Paul Tillich said in a sermon, is that the Messiah was "born in a grave." Those who skip Thursday and Friday but show up on Easter Sunday are missing the essential truth of the passion. They also bypass the profound grief that attends Jesus's death. But there's more to it than that. They have also missed one of the most important lessons he taught before dying. During Holy Week Jesus teaches the art of losing.

In the first three stanzas of her poem "One Art," Elizabeth Bishop ruminates on life's reductions:

> The art of losing isn't hard to master;
> so many things seem filled with the intent
> to be lost that their loss is no disaster.
>
> Lose something every day. Accept the fluster
> of lost door keys, the hour badly spent.
> The art of losing isn't hard to master.
>
> Then practice losing farther, losing faster:
> places, and names, and where it was you meant
> to travel. None of these will bring disaster.

The poem is heavy with irony. That Bishop would label the inevitable slippages of time and memory an "art" is downright funny. And that she would equate our desperate responses to loss with the notion of mastery reeks of self-deception. When you are slammed by tragedy, what is there "to master"? By the last stanza, however, the poet has narrowed her loss to a beloved person, and only then arrives at an honest response:

—Even losing you (the joking voice, a gesture
I love) I shan't have lied. It's evident
the art of losing's not too hard to master
though it may look like (*Write* it!) like disaster.*

What Jesus offers this Holy Week is not an escape from loss but a better way of losing. In each passion account, and especially in the Gospel of John, Jesus suffers humiliation and defeat but does not relinquish his identity as the Son of God. His final cry is addressed to his Father. His divinity is confirmed not by coming down from the cross but by his gestures of love while impaled upon it. From the cross he provides for his mother and forgives his tormentors. From the cross he draws a world of lost souls to himself. As it turns out, what remains in each of us is not the bravado of mastery but the vulnerability of love.

All our losses, however sharp or permanent they may be, deprive us of our ability to think and act beyond ourselves. They rob us of the very quality of love Jesus performed in the Upper Room and on the cross. Take grief, for example. Grief bears witness to no story or solution larger than itself. It shrinks your life to the exact size of your longing. The art of love is lost to you.

By God's power, however, some manage to break through the anguish and, in the midst of their own loss, find someone else to help or love. A boy dies of a drug overdose, and his parents take a new and active role in drug education for teens. A woman survives breast cancer, but instead of nesting with her own anxiety, she reaches out to other women with the same disease. Poor people help other poor people. The bereaved understand and comfort the bereaved. This is the true art of losing. And it is an art or, as the apostle would say, a gift of the Spirit, no less a blessing than any of the other, better-known gifts. Jesus teaches the art of losing. It's one of the reasons why some of us will sit in a darkening church on a Thursday night.

* From *The Complete Poems, 1927–1979*, by Elizabeth Bishop. Copyright 1979, 1983 by Alice Helen Methfessel. Reprinted by permission of Farrar, Straus & Giroux.

6

HE WAS FORSAKEN

And about three o'clock Jesus cried with a loud voice, "Eli, Eli, lema sabachthani?" that is, "My God, my God, why have you forsaken me?"

—MATTHEW 27:46

According to the four evangelists, Jesus spoke seven times from the cross. In one gospel he expresses his love for his mother, in another his compassion for his executioners. He promises paradise to a criminal. At the last, he commends his spirit to God and triumphantly announces the completion of his mission. In the Gospel of John, he rules from the cross and dies like a king.

In the Gospel of Matthew, however, Jesus speaks from the cross but one time, and that in Hebrew. It is not a grand word. It is not a word to inspire or instruct. Jesus is engulfed in the chaos of dying. He is suspended in darkness. He cannot see. He cannot breathe. In Matthew, his life ends not with the exclamation point of victory but, as many lives end, with a question mark. In his cry the human spirit is broken down to its most basic unit of anguish—*Why?* "My God, my God, why have you forsaken me?"

The church calls it his cry of dereliction—*dereliction*—a terrible word. A derelict ship is one that is about to sink. The men and even the rats have abandoned it to the gale. A derelict lying on some doorway or in an alley is a lost soul.

Some years ago, a scholar named Oscar Cullmann wrote a comparative study of the death of Socrates and the death of Jesus. He was not the first to do so. The early opponents of Christianity often made this comparison to the detriment of Jesus and the Christian faith. You may remember that when the Greek philosopher Socrates is condemned to die, he drinks the hemlock with great serenity. In the face of death and with no god to call on, Socrates coolly discusses the pros and cons of immortality with composure and reasonableness. He dies the way you and I would like to die. With dignity. The divinity school next door houses a center for the study of medicine and religion. It brings together the disciplines of medicine, sociology, and theology in order to help provide the terminally ill with a good death. A death like Socrates's.

When we turn to the death of Jesus, however, we must admit it's nothing like a philosopher's death. In the Garden of Gethsemane, Mark says he was shaking. Matthew says he threw himself to the ground. Luke reports that sweat fell from his brow like great drops of blood. He doesn't want this thing to happen. Doesn't want to drink the cup. Doesn't want to be alone. "Can't you watch with me if only for one hour?" he complains to his friends. When the end comes, it comes in the heartbreak of abandonment.

There are ways of softening this picture, of course. We have methods of making the death of Jesus less *terrible* and more endurable, the way bad religious art smooths the rough edges of real life. The words "My God, my God, why have you forsaken me?" constitute the first sentence of Psalm 22. Some have asked, isn't it possible that Jesus, the pious Jew, is simply reciting a verse he had known since childhood—the way dying people sometimes revert to the words that formed them in their youth—the way a dying person who hasn't spoken for days may blurt out the Lord's Prayer—the way a ninety-five-year-old in the nursing home suddenly recites, "Now I lay me down to sleep"?

Listen to Psalm 22. It reads like a blueprint for crucifixion:

> All who see me mock at me;
>> they make mouths at me, they shake their heads;
>> "Commit your cause to the Lord;

let him deliver—let him rescue the one
in whom he delights!" ...
 For dogs are all around me;
 a company of evildoers encircles me.
They have pierced my hands and feet—
I can count all my bones.

Yet by the end, the psalmist comes around to a magnificent statement of hope and trust in the Lord. "Posterity will serve him; future generations will be told about the Lord, / and proclaim his deliverance to a people yet unborn."

So, isn't it at least possible (or so goes the argument) that Jesus *intended* to pray the whole psalm, including its hope-filled conclusion? You see what I'm getting at: He wasn't really abandoned, nor did he feel totally forsaken. He meant to pray the whole psalm. He simply died before he could complete it.

This interpretation opens the way to a happier crucifixion and a less mysterious God. Perhaps Jesus didn't suffer quite as much as we thought he did. Or perhaps he only suffered in his physical nature or as a human being. Some first-century spiritualists taught that a divine part of him floated above that hideous scene at Golgotha, untouched by its fear and pain.

Such thoughts make it easier to think about a beautiful death. Socrates was right. There's nothing to be afraid of! When Saint Paul called death "the last enemy to be destroyed," or when the poet Dylan Thomas wrote to his dying father, "Do not go gentle into that good night / Rage, rage, against the dying of the light," he must have been depressed or having a bad day, because death is as natural as life.

But if that's the case, why this cry of dereliction? Why this "abandon ship" if the ship is not really going to sink?

There's an old saying about Jesus that casts light on our question. An ancient theologian said, "What he did not assume, he does not redeem." Which means: if there is any part of this human condition that Jesus didn't take on himself, then that part is left outside redemption. What he did not assume he does not redeem.

Have you ever been tempted? So was he. Your temptations have been redeemed in his. Have you ever been hated or treated as an outcast? So was he. You have a place in him. Have you ever been lonely, afraid, or without a place called home? Have you ever had doubts not only about yourself but about God, whether God cares about you or knows your name? Have you ever cried when you're sad? Do you sweat when you are scared? *So did he! So did he!* Even that which is most hidden in you and most difficult to express—your despair—has been shouldered by him like a heavy burden. You have a place in him.

At Christmas, we celebrated God's appearance in the flesh. We read Matthew then too; Matthew, who calls Jesus *Immanuel*, God with us. But then we were conjuring an adorable baby. Good Friday also reveals *Immanuel* but with a saving vengeance. On this day, we begin to fathom the full extent of the words "flesh" and "with us."

Jesus is the baby all right: he is the one abandoned in the dumpster. He's also the scared and pregnant teenager. He's the jobless guy loitering on East Main. His manger is an AIDS (or a COVID-19) ward. His cross is a refugee camp. He is a suicidal teenager. He is *you* at your lowest pulse. As low as hell itself. For you, he has gone derelict.

You may ask, was Jesus really abandoned by God or did he only *feel* abandoned? Good question, a profound question, in fact, but one that is too deep for me. Your preacher is like the guide in uncharted territory who says, "This is as far as I go. You're on your own."

There have been bolder guides, of course. Saint John of the Cross, who experienced the believer's dark night of the soul. Or Martin Luther, who spoke tremblingly of the "hidden God." Then there was Dietrich Bonhoeffer, who prophesied that the people of his generation might have to live as if there were no God (as if God were not a "given") but always in the presence of God! And don't forget: Bonhoeffer wrote that desperate sentence not from his study in the university but from his cell in a concentration camp.

Jesus was forsaken by God. There, I've said it (even though I don't understand it). The one who promised Israel, "I will never leave you or forsake you," forsook his own son. And like the aggrieved child he was, the son cried out in protest—against his own Father.

That's a start for you and me. When we are plunged into a deep place and feel abandoned by God, we too will cry out—but to God! We may even feel that we are praying desperately to a divine Absence, like children crying in the dark.

But I say, go ahead: *Rage, rage against the dying of the light*, in the name of him who for your sake cried out, "My God, my God, why . . ."

7

BURIED

*And so, because it was the Jewish day of Preparation, and
the tomb was nearby, they laid Jesus there.*

—JOHN 19:31–42

During Holy Week we all become children again. Children are the
most orderly of creatures. Every night they expect the same stories to
be repeated, and in the same order. No detail is too small or lacking in
significance. And nothing may be changed or omitted. The adopted
child says, "Then, of all the children you chose me, right?" There are
parts of Jesus's story we wouldn't mind skipping, but, no, we are not
allowed. We need to hear it all: "He suffered under Pontius Pilate,
was crucified, died—and was buried."

"Buried" is the dispensable word at the end of the sentence. It's
where the voice drops beneath the threshold of hope and we swallow
the last word, not wanting to imagine it and never really appreciat-
ing the finality of its power. I understand why morticians wait until
the family has departed before closing the grave. There is no way to
cosmeticize that act. It makes a mockery of the long-stemmed roses.
For the one being buried is now being segregated from the beauty
of life and the vitalities that sustain the planet. The theologian Karl
Barth captures the irrelevance of the dead when he writes, "We shall
be buried. Someday a company of men will proceed out to a church-
yard and lower a coffin and everyone will go home; but one will not
come back, and that will be me. . . . They will bury me as a thing that
is superfluous and disturbing in the land of the living."

With the first shovelful of earth the forgetting begins. Little gifts and distinctions we call "personality" are gradually worn smooth. I don't know my great-grandmother's first name. I don't know my great-grandfather's profession, or if he had one. What's worse, I don't know what sort of people they were. Years ago, when your folks added the patio in the garden, you wrote your initials in the fresh concrete. The house is for sale now. Who will know or care how much you loved that place and those days? Who will interpret your memorial to yourself?

Buried. In the Gospel of John Jesus dies pronouncing his mission accomplished. "It is finished," he cries. But at that point we are not sped away in a black limo. There is more. We get the clinical report of the soldier's rude autopsy conducted with a spear. We watch them take him down and, finally, we see him sealed away. This probing with the spear the church interpreted as the water of baptism and the blood of communion. Augustine remarks, "This is a different kind of corpse. For out of a dead man comes life." But take away the symbolism, and you are left with the gruesome details. Must we see all this? And why? Isn't it enough to hear the words "*It* is finished"? Must we *see* him finished?

Jesus is given a burial befitting one who has reigned from the cross. He is laid in a pristine tomb, wrapped in linen strips that have been soaked in aromatic oils, and packed in one hundred pounds of deodorizing spices. The burial ritual says two things about him: Jesus was a king, and Jesus is dead.

In *The Shaking of the Foundations*, theologian Paul Tillich tells the story of a witness at the Nuremberg war-crime trials who had escaped a death camp by hiding in a grave in a Jewish cemetery. While he was there, he saw a young woman in a nearby grave giving birth to a child. She was assisted by an aged gravedigger wrapped in a linen shroud. When the newborn uttered its first cry, the old man looked to heaven and prayed, "Great God, hast Thou finally sent the Messiah to us? For who else than the Messiah himself can be born in a grave?"

Who indeed? Who but the Messiah can transform the tomb into a womb of new life and hope? We *must* see the entombment. We must confess him *buried* so we can see more clearly the God who raises the dead. The burial of Jesus is the most eloquent testimony we have to the creative power of God. Just as God created Adam from the dust of the earth, so God re-creates the whole human race from the sickening sweet remains of his dead son. This is the God about whom Paul says in 1 Corinthians, "He has chosen things low and contemptible, mere nothings, to overthrow the existing order." The burial of Jesus is testimony to God. Only God's Messiah can be born in the grave.

Christianity offers no easy solution to death. For death is woven into the fabric of our lives and the life of the planet. Rather, by graphically demonstrating the finality of death, God uses it to manifest his power, the way the master magician makes sure we've seen his assistant in the box before sawing it in half.

The early Christians in Rome, whose religious meetings were prohibited, tried to trick the authorities by calling themselves "burial societies." There's some truth to the name. For we consider ourselves buried with Jesus and therefore stripped of every pretense of self-sufficiency. His burial invites us to examine every sort of decomposition that assails us, including the final one, and then to trust that what God did for the Buried One he will do for us.

This is the promise of Good Friday. Thanks to his burial, there is hope at ours. Because of him, we can say at an open grave, "In sure and certain hope of the resurrection to eternal life through our Lord Jesus Christ, we commend to almighty God our sister; and we commit her body to the ground." Our orderly confession, "He was crucified, died, and was buried," isn't a litany of despair. It leads us to the crowning point of the story:

The King is dead! Long live the King!

8

HOLY SATURDAY IN A TIME OF PLAGUE

On the sabbath they rested according to the commandment.

—LUKE 23:56B

Holy Saturday is no one's favorite religious holiday. It lacks the darkness and the drama of a dying Savior. Nor is it bathed in light to celebrate a risen Lord. Its color is a liminal gray.

But it's where we are, all of us. It is our new season. A virus, I am told, is not a life-form but is sheathed in life. Although it is not alive, it anticipates life or, as one virologist writes, it is an organism "at the edge of life."

In its own way Holy Saturday, too, rests just at the edge of life, the life of the risen Christ. But for now, it is a very quiet day. When I was a boy, I was always outraged that the world could be so busy and noisy a place while Jesus was resting in his tomb. Today it is different. Today, it's as if the whole world—my world, at least—is observing a regimen of silence in honor of the Lord's burial.

In Wuhan and San Francisco and Atlanta and St. Louis the streets are empty, or at least less traveled. In the rural buffer where I live (a liminal space between a university and surrounding farmland), our road is quieter than usual. No one misses street noise, but it is spring, and I miss the music blasting through our campus, the sounds of laughter and the murmur of learned conversations from tables along the sidewalks.

After the horrors of Good Friday, Saturday is a day of decompression and reflection. For years my mother told me how her thirty-year-old mother, Elizabeth, died in the flu pandemic of 1918, how she almost recovered, then relapsed and died in her bedroom. In one inexplicable stroke it rendered her a motherless child. I never felt the full force of her loss until these endless days. Now I can feel it in my bones.

In a time of pandemic, our new season of Holy Saturday invites us to reexamine our spiritual bearings when, as Psalm 46 says, the kingdoms are tottering, the earth is melting, and desolations threaten the earth. "Be still and know that I am God." The command sounds harsh, but it is not a rebuke. It is an invitation to enter the supernatural stillness of God. It means, "Don't be afraid of what comes next."

The Gospels say little about the disciples' behavior on Holy Saturday. We can only imagine. It was a day of rest. They were required by law to stay home and rest. What preparations the women made must have been done furtively.

In the world of the coronavirus, we are also waiting. But waiting for what? When the women came to the tomb in the gray morning, they came not with high hopes but with their world's version of embalming fluid. In our time of contagion, with the toll of fatalities doubling every few days, our waiting does not appear to be enriched by hope any more than theirs was.

Our waiting has an intransitive feel. "For what?" is hard to answer. For it to be over. For those who are sick to recover. For a magically resurrected economy. For school to start and the multiplex to open. For baseball. For a paycheck once again. Waiting to get back to where we were—which for many of us was not a good place to begin with. The people who clean hotel rooms, who work at Macy's or Gap or the diner down the block, whose husbands or wives, parents or grandparents, have died alone and are mourned—virtually, who live in the contagion of prisons, who are waiting for a bed in the ICU— what are they hoping for?

But waiting, like hoping, demands an object. We are waiting for a solution to the inexplicable. We are waiting for deliverance from our vulnerability to nature, of course—and from death—but even more from the misinformation, hoarding, anxiety, and loneliness that make the pandemic even worse. Which is to say, we want to be delivered from ourselves.

Our season of Holy Saturday is also a time of caring for others. We are FaceTiming, Zooming, and Skyping with friends and family. We are also looking out for neighbors we haven't seen in a while and loosening our wallets for those who can no longer clean our houses or clear our gutters. Two days ago, I got a beautiful letter from a parishioner I cared for forty-two years ago. Now she is caring for me. It's the pandemic, to be sure, but it's also the season of Holy Saturday, a time to reflect on the blessings of friendship, marriage, community, and hope.

In a time of pandemic, conspiracy theories go viral and new ethical issues arise unbidden. How can we know the truth? Which authority shall we trust? The president? The CDC? Fox News? How shall we balance personal safety and economic health? What are the ethics of taking chances with other people's lives? Is it right to profit from the pandemic? How can we make sure that treatment of the rich doesn't override care for the poor? Who gets the last ventilator? The first vaccine?

The moral questions are not new. In 1527 the bubonic plague returned to the city of Wittenberg, Germany. It was a recurrence of the scourge that had killed more than a third of Europe's population in the fourteenth century. As the religious leader of his community, Martin Luther was obliged to address the question, May one flee the city in a time of plague?

Luther counseled the government to establish centralized hospitals to avoid the contamination of individual homes and to move the cemeteries outside the city. In words that sound familiar to us, he wrote, "Then I shall fumigate, help purify the air, administer medicine, and take it. I shall avoid places and persons where my presence is not needed in order not to become contaminated and thus perchance infect and pollute others." Plague answers the question, "Who is my neighbor?" Pastors should remain with their flock. Luther stayed.

Today his advice is being followed by doctors, nurses, technicians, and other workers who are braving the coronavirus that others may live. As Luther would put it, they are the "little Christs" in our midst.

We believe that the Good Shepherd participates in this plague and subjects himself to its suffering and anxiety. The Gospels do not sugarcoat his fear in Gethsemane or his suffering on the cross. He even sojourned in the wasteland of Holy Saturday on our behalf.

The suffering of Jesus was especially vivid for people living in the Middle Ages. They knew firsthand the horrors of sickness, childbirth, medical care, death, and the local burial pit. They could identify. The crucified God was their only refuge.

It is within this frame that we meet the mystic and anchoress Julian of Norwich. The plague of 1348–1349 remains a relatively fresh memory in East Anglia. Julian is desperately ill on her bed, struggling to breathe and preparing to die. The priest has been called. As he intones the final blessing, he holds a crucifix before her eyes.

Then a strange thing happens.

The figure on the cross begins to bleed, shedding great stalactites of blood and mucus. In an image shocking for its sensuousness, Julian compares the blood to water dripping from the eaves of a house and to strips of herring flayed at her kitchen sink.

Later, when she describes Jesus's dead body, with its pustules and blue-blackened color, she is giving a clinical picture of something everyone in Norwich and in all of England would have immediately recognized.

It is the picture of a man who is willing to catch the very disease that he cures, who visits a young woman's house in a time of plague and, while healing her, dies of it himself.

Like Julian, we know there is more to come. The best-known line of her *Revelations* is this: "But all shall be well, and all manner of things shall be well."

But my favorite occurs several chapters later, when the Lord says, "You shall not be overcome."

Waiting in Hope

9

I HAVE SEEN THE FUTURE

"See, the home of God is among mortals. He will dwell with them; . . . he will wipe every tear from their eyes. Death will be no more; mourning and crying and pain will be no more, for the first things have passed away." And the one who was seated on the throne said, "See, I am making all things new."

—MALACHI 4:1–5; REVELATION 21:3–5

Each in his own way, the prophet and the seer, speaks words that we desperately need to take into our hearts. Each says, "I have seen the future, and it belongs to God."*

With Advent exactly two weeks away, the whole Christian church imperceptibly begins to lean forward and to yearn for the coming of God. The lessons read today are not specially chosen for this congregation but represent the whole church's rhythm of faith. For many here today, that yearning for God and a greater revelation is focused by the death of Amy Elizabeth, a member of this choir and a sister in the body of Jesus Christ. It is good that we have these lessons, so the whole church can minister to us. It is good that we have dancers and drums today, because much of what we feel cannot be spoken

---

* This sermon was preached on the second-last Sunday of the church year. That week a Duke undergraduate student was killed in a bus accident on campus. On Sunday a troupe of liturgical dancers and percussionists performed solemnly and triumphantly in Duke Chapel.

but only danced and furiously drummed. What words we sing will stick in our throats. What words we speak will be nothing more than a groan of faith in the God who is Alpha and Omega, the beginning and the end.

God will come: so say the prophet and the seer. Not as a baby anymore, but God will come in quite a different way to set all things right. In the meantime, we dance and drum, sing and weep, not only because a precious eighteen-year-old has died, but because after the dying and the crying, God comes.

Most people imagine a God who occupies more of the past than the future. God seems to fit right in in museums with temple friezes, ancient manuscripts, the Old Masters. That is God's domain. When we think of God, our minds drift back to childhood, when those Bible stories and Sunday school lessons created a world in which we had a place. "O God of my youth," the poet prayed. When you think about your time in this university, isn't it more comfortable for you to remember the familiar people and events that brought you to this place than it is to contemplate the riddle of what awaits you as you leave? The past has a face. The future—and today we must say, death—is without form or face.

But precisely here, where life is hardest and most inscrutable, Christianity speaks a word into the void. It proclaims a future that has contours and form, and even a face. The God of the Bible, who in the New Testament is known as the Father of Jesus Christ, turns out to be a God of the future. The past, for all its vastness, isn't nearly large enough a place for all that God promises to be for Amy and for all who have preceded us in death. Only God can care for both the past and the future.

When I was a grade schooler, a boy in my class drowned. I remember very little about it except that it had a profound effect on me. I couldn't eat or sleep properly or concentrate in school. A few days ago, doubtless prompted by Amy's tragic death, my mind went back to that event, and I was shocked to realize that for the life of me I couldn't remember the boy's name. That's the fear, isn't it? When you, her classmates, are old and gray, who will remember Amy Eliz-abeth's name and cherish her as a person? Who will remember those who are appointed to remember such things? And when we are all gone, who will remember us?

When it comes to remembering, we are not particularly accom-plished, but God is. But God—*God*—gathers the jagged fragments of life, the tragedies and losses, the murky memories—writes down all the names, and none is forgotten, not one. When the Israelites were in exile, they feared, understandably, that they would be assim-ilated into the nations and lost to history and the memory of God. God said to Israel through the prophet Isaiah, "Can a woman forget her nursing child? . . . Even these may forget, yet I will not forget you. See, I have inscribed you on the palms of my hands."

Malachi and the seer paint two very different scenarios for the future but each with the same lead actor, God. And each with a vi-sion marked by the simple imperative: *See*. Malachi, the unknown prophet, was ministering to a depressed people recently returned from exile. Israel as a nation-state was gone; the temple was noth-ing. Because they had no future, they were hurting, and hurting one another. The book of Malachi reveals something about the nature of God we had forgotten or repressed.

The Old Testament does not end with a beatific vision but with a burst of rage. "*See*, the day is coming, burning like an oven, when all the arrogant and all evildoers will be stubble; the day that comes shall burn them up, says the LORD of hosts." As it turns out, the God of the future is not the shadowy, benign presence we had imagined but a God who takes sides and says, "I am fed up with suffering and hunger, two-bit tyrants, and evildoers. I will have my day." In the prophet's own words, this is a God who is capable of uttering the sentence "I hate."

The preacher William Sloane Coffin once said in this pulpit, "If you love the good but do not hate evil, you are doomed to sen-timentality." But a God who hates? When our son was a very little person, one of our family projects was to train him not to say "hate."

We had nice little talks about it: "This is a word that is not worthy of you," we said (and by the way, that's an argument that doesn't work particularly well with a four-year-old). "You didn't learn to say 'hate' in Sunday school," we said, "not from Jesus." We never let him read Malachi—"Jacob have I loved; Esau I have hated." Or Amos—"I hate, I despise your feasts." Or Isaiah—"I hate robbery and wrong." Or even the psalmist—"The Lord loves those who hate evil." We are tempted to say to God, "This is a word that is unworthy of you."

But the prophet insists that some things are worthy of God's rage, and ours. If you can visit the concentration camp in Dachau and enter by the same gate through which so many prisoners passed, and if you can run your hand over the terrible lie that is carved in the wrought iron: *Arbeit Macht Frei*, Work Will Make You Free, and not feel something like rage, then listen again to Malachi's God. If you can see the aged faces on the bodies of children in Somalia without feeling rage—not only at the governments of the world, who can deliver bombs but not food, but also at the sheer senselessness of the suffering of innocents—then listen again to the prophet's God. When an unsuspecting young woman is lost on her way to class for no reason at all, you can almost hear Malachi's God say, "I hate that my dear child has died."

The Gospel of Mark tells us that one day Jesus was confronted by a man covered with sores and putrid flesh who cried out, "Jesus, make me clean." "Moved with pity, he stretched out his hand and touched him." What scholars take as the original wording of Jesus's reply, however, is very mysterious. Reliable manuscripts read, "And Jesus, moved with *anger*, touched him." No one knows the meaning of that reaction, but might we understand it as God's own rage at the insult to a good creation?

And what of John the Seer's scenario? A *see-er* sees on behalf of others. From the Apocalypse we learn something more about God. The God of the Apocalypse heals our wounds, dries our tears, and promises to minister to us forever. "I have seen the future," says John, "and death, suffering, and weeping will have no part in it." The God of Malachi cuts through evil like a blowtorch; Malachi's God rages with us in our grief. When we turn to the book of Revelation, the anger seems to dissipate. There we see the saints gathered around the throne, and among them high and lifted up is not the angry warrior we might have expected, but the Lamb. The Lamb is in the midst of them. What does it mean to us in this terrible moment, that at the crown of reality sits not a symbol of death or retribution—not the Grim Reaper or the Terminator—but something altogether beyond our imagining?

This morning we have come to church filled with questions. That's not unusual. Most of our questions begin with "Why?" But this one is different. This morning we are asking about hope. The grief is so powerful, we can only ask, "Is there any hope to which we are entitled?" Both Malachi and John the Seer offer us hope in God, but in different ways. The God who thundered over Palestine in Malachi's day is the same one who watched his Son go to the cross in solidarity with all who suffer. We may hope in the God who raised Jesus from death.

Jesus was one of the exiles, lost and without a future. He was Amy Elizabeth, gone before her time. Jesus was like us when we are lost. Who will keep searching for us? Who will remember us? "This is how I will remember you," says our God, "the same way I remembered my Son—by raising him up."

This gospel is not a problem solver, it's a promise. We have God's word that the slaughtered, the starving, our sister, and all who are slipping away from us are not meant to be discarded or forgotten and will not be. It's a sign that they—and we—are meant to be more, not less, than we are, that even death, as authoritative and final as it seems, is not the last word.

God's first and last word to us is a promise of life. That life is signified in Jesus's triumph over the grave. It's based on Jesus's own testimony, given in this our darkest hour: "I have seen the future," he says, "and it is as cold and hard as a tomb. And as glorious as the saints in heaven."

Anyone can say it, dear friends. You don't have to be a prophet or a preacher, but only a person of faith: I have seen the future. And its name is Jesus.

IO

The Dream of Arrival

Then Joseph got up, took the the child [Jesus] and his mother by night, and went to Egypt, and remained there until the death of Herod.

—LUKE 2:1–20; MATTHEW 2:1–23

When all was still, and it was midnight, thine almighty Word, O Lord, descended from the royal throne.

—WISDOM OF SOLOMON 18:15
ANTIPHON, CHRISTMAS VESPERS

And now we come to the hardest work of Christmas. What, you thought the hard work was done? You thought the hard work was finished in choosing the gifts, baking the cookies, cleaning the house, watching the diet, and otherwise surviving what one journalist calls "our annual ordeal of fun"? You thought the hard work was getting yourself or someone you love through the loneliness of this season that is only magnified by its artificial gaiety? You thought the hard work was reassembling your family like a stubborn jigsaw puzzle in the hope that all the pieces would fit together and stay together, if only for two or three days?

No, the hardest work of Christmas is believing that it's all true.

It would be as if a great emperor should summon his son to his chamber. When the young man arrives, the emperor whispers a secret message in his ear and sends him on a long and perilous journey. But

first the young man must traverse the anterooms and vestibules surrounding the throne and descend a great staircase, which is swarming
with the comings and goings of lesser officials, servants, and suppli-
cants. After that, there will be a courtyard and then another, followed
by inner walls, and other staircases, all equally clotted with humanity,
and still he will not have penetrated the outer wall of the palace.
But the messenger is strong and tireless and bears on his breast the
seal of the emperor. Now leaving the palace, he must fight his way
through the teeming streets of the city and then across vast and dangerous landscapes toward his destination in a foreign land.

How is it possible, you have every right to ask, that *one* messenger, bearing the secrets of the emperor, could ever pierce such an
impossible density and come—to *you*? But you gather with others by
candlelight with the midwinter wind howling and, against all odds,
dream it to be true.*

We are the community of the dream, and this is our season. For at
the heart of the Christian hope is the stubborn belief in the emperor,
the son, and the message. At Christmas we insist that a message has
reached us from the throne of God and, more than a message, a divine
person. We also believe that the journey is perennial; not only does
it happen every year for us, but it has infinite powers of extension to
any person or community anywhere in the world. The dream is so real
that we have erected great churches in which this message is taught
and celebrated. And most important, each of us believes that, despite
daily obstructions to the contrary, the divine messenger has found his
way to us with a word of hope. And so, with Mary, who "pondered all
these things in her heart," and the shepherds, who were willing to make
their own journey to Bethlehem, we dream the Dream of Arrival.

From a human perspective, it almost didn't happen. The parents
were so poor. They were living in an occupied region of the world.
Only with great difficulty did they obey the government's command

---

* With apologies to Franz Kafka, "An Imperial Message," in *The Basic
Kafka* (New York: Pocket Books, 1979).

to be registered. Their baby was born in a stable, as Luther wrote, "no crib for a bed." It's almost impossible for us to penetrate the veneer of tradition to the abject poverty and rampant violence into which our Lord was born.

The Gospel of Matthew adds the story of Herod's murderous intent and the Holy Family's flight into Egypt. The gospel reminds us that their roles are inverted. Herod is in his royal palace; Jesus and his family are on the run. The First Family is a refugee family. They are forced into refugee status by the threats of a paranoid tyrant, who in his rage has his goon squads kill all the boy babies of Bethlehem. When Joseph and his family finally return to Palestine, they resettle in the north for fear of the king's son, Archelaus.

We can sharpen our imagination of the first Christmas by attending to the plight of refugees in our midst and around the world. Equally important, we can better understand the plight of contemporary refugees by meditating on the events surrounding the birth of our refugee Lord. Everywhere, it seems, in the Middle East, Asia, Africa, and the Americas, people are on the move in dangerous migrations toward unknown destinations. With the prophet, their cry rises from the camps, "O that thou wouldst rend the heavens and come down!" They too dream of an Arrival marked by peace and safety. They too dream of gathering their children around them and celebrating a holy time with their family. With them, we pray, "Bless all the poor children in thy tender care." How appropriate that the young people who were brought to this country as immigrants are called "Dreamers."

Before the Christmas story can bathe us in its own warmth, we must see it for what it is, the story of a displaced family chosen and protected by God to redeem a broken world. The almighty God chooses to "arrive" by means of a poor baby. But as the writer Frederick Buechner remarks, once you've found God in a manger, you can find him anywhere. We may speak of "the magic of Christmas," but what we mean (and hope for) is the peace of Christ. It can happen anywhere.

More than a hundred years ago, on Christmas Eve, British and German soldiers along the western front spontaneously put down their guns and crossed the lines to greet one another. They exchanged gifts and food and cigarettes and performed joint burial ceremonies. Some played soccer. The Great Christmas Truce, as it is called, lasted about a day until senior officers forbade the peace, and the killing resumed in earnest. The Great Truce teaches many things. It tells us how desperately we dream of peace and how demonically the powers of war oppose it. In our own moments of Christmas Truce, it reminds us how difficult it will be to *keep* the peace of this night, how easily it will slip away from us. That is, unless, after the wreaths are stored away and the tree has been discarded, the message and the Messenger are allowed to remain.

If not, there will never be enough Christmas to go around. The good cheer will fall short of holiday projections, the preacher's words won't measure up to seasonal demand, the new year will *loom* rather than beckon. December is the cruelest month, if what you wanted for Christmas was not a returnable gift, but something more closely related to what God intended to give. Which is peace and salvation. It's hard to settle for a blender or a new sweater when you were hoping for a better friendship with your brother, or acceptance by your parents for who you really are.

Some of you can remember seventy-five Christmases or more—seventy-five Arrivals of hope. We evaluate our Christmases past by remembering how deeply the presence of Jesus penetrated our hearts or enriched our relationships. On a Christmas long ago, my wife and I had no gifts for each other but a new baby. So, we tied a ribbon round her ankle, put her in her carry cot, and placed her under the tree, our only present. In the absence of the things and obligations with which we have since cluttered up our holidays, this was one of our better Christmases, maybe the best: the gift of a child, and nothing more.

At times like these, believing in the Christmas gospel isn't hard at all. It's *keeping* it that's the challenge. For the soldiers on the western

front, it lasted a day. And for us? If believing in Christmas is only
a feeling or a break in our schedule, it won't last long. One thing
is certain: in a world engulfed in war and suffering, children will
continue to be born. To a church that yearns for a powerful leader
only the poor child will continue to arrive in his place. And Jesus
will be enough.

Incredible as it may seem, the Messenger has fought his way
through all obstacles, including death itself, and has arrived. He has
been born among you this very Christmas. The communion we've
been waiting for is here. Soon we will taste it. There is enough to go
around. Like a new baby, it's a dream come true.

It is Christmas Day 1521. Martin Luther is too sick to go to church.
So, a group of parishioners goes to his house, where he preaches the
Christmas gospel with incomparable power and beauty. In it he re-
tells the story in the idiom of his day, rendering Mary and Joseph and
the shepherds as down-to-earth and ordinary as a group of German
peasants.

Then he deftly magnifies the simple scene and gives it cosmic significance. He asks us to imagine the Christ child in a manger bathed
in light at the center of an otherwise darkened stage. The manger is
surrounded by enemies and the forces of evil. "All else is darkness,"
he says dramatically, "save for this child." Then, as if to pierce the veil
that always exists between the storyteller and his audience, he leans
into his listeners, including us, and issues a challenge: "Now, if this is
all true, and it is true, let everything else go." And you and I, yearning
for such a promise, are sorely tempted to do just that.

What if it's *all* true—the emperor, the journey, the baby, the
arrival? What *if*? If it is, then for the dream's sake, let everything
else go.

II

What May I Hope?

> I wait for the LORD, my soul waits,
>   and in his word I hope;
> my soul waits for the Lord
>   more than those who watch for
>   the morning,
>   more than those who watch for
>   the morning.
>
> —PSALM 130:5–6

It was like a tomb on Friday evening when we gathered in this place. A single candle sent spooky shadows up the walls. We sang, "*Were you there when they laid him in the tomb?*" And perhaps because we are more intimately acquainted with death than with resurrection, we felt that we were *there*.

There is a final, unfamiliar stanza to the Negro spiritual. It goes like this:

> Were you there when he rose up from the dead?
> Were you there when he rose up from the dead?
> O, sometimes it causes me to tremble, tremble.
> Were you there when he rose up from the dead?

Despite our best efforts to re-create that scene historically or liturgically—with a bank of spring flowers or worship at sunrise—we might as well admit it: no, we were *not* there. Nobody was. The most important event in the history of the world took place off-camera, just outside the "laws" of history. It was transacted not between armies or diplomats but between God the Father and God the Son by the power of God the Holy Spirit.

It happened in darkness.

We don't know if it was a typically warm Palestinian morning or if it was unseasonably cool. We don't know if the sky thundered or if it was preternaturally still. And depending on which of the four Gospels you read, it was an angel or a young man or two men who met the women at the tomb. And how many women were there? The number varies from one to three, and most of them were named Mary.

We don't know what he *looked* like when he was no longer dead—whether he burst from the tomb in heavenly light or came out the way Lazarus had, slowly unwrapping his bandages and squinting with wonder at the dawn.

All these things and more, we don't know.

Someone should have debriefed those Roman soldiers. I have a feeling somebody did. They probably said what Mary said, or Lazarus, or anyone who has experienced the power of God: "It causes me to tremble."

A great philosopher [Immanuel Kant] once said there are only three questions worth asking: What can I know? What ought I to do? What may I hope? With all due respect to the first two, it is the Third Question that's on our minds today. It's the Third Question that keeps us awake at night and gets us up in the morning.

The questions appear in descending order: first, the all-important question of knowledge (what exactly happened?), then the question of ethical action or duty (what should I do about it?), and when none of these satisfies our deepest desires, we turn to hope. The Third Question is so tentative it's almost pitiful. Given what I know about my own heart and the crushing reality of death, what little crumb of hope am I permitted? Hope as desert. Hope as booby prize.

The question of hope, however, is as realistic as the first two.

A concerned mother asks the same question as her child enters treatment for a severe birth defect: Which therapeutic avenues are closing, which are still open? Given the severity of the prognosis, what am I permitted to hope? She poses the question to some physician or therapist every day. There is no way she can know the answer. She has no letter from the future that permits her to *see* her daughter, with the aid of a personal assistant, entering college as a bright and promising member of the freshman class.

It won't surprise you to know that the Hebrew word for "hope" can also mean "wait." "I wait for the Lord, and in his word do I hope." The word for hope doesn't appear in any of the four Gospels. As a verb it occurs most famously in Luke 24 where the two disciples on the road to Emmaus speak of hope as if it were a thing of the past: "We had hoped."

Only in Paul do we see a developing theology of hope, one that emerges from his proclamation of the resurrection of Jesus. He goes so far as to claim that we are saved by hope, with the commonsense caveat, "Hope that is seen is not hope." If you have the final results in front of you, you have moved into a different category. But, Paul adds, "If we hope for what we do *not* see, we *wait* for it with patience."

On my only visit to Africa, there was a great drought in the land. Whenever I mentioned it to my new Zimbabwean acquaintances, they didn't chat about the weather as we Midwesterners like to do, but they invariably responded with a serenity that eludes me: "We are waiting for the rain." Our culture (which means you and me) is not gifted when it comes to waiting. But in Holy Week we practice it with great precision. We reenact the six hours of his dying. We see him sorrowfully laid in the tomb. We leave the church in silence with no speaking to others, not even in the parking lot.

But then on what some call "Holy Saturday" we loosen up a bit and things return to what we call "normal." We get the tires rotated in the morning, take the kids to soccer practice, eat half of a pizza, watch part of a movie, loiter at the farmers' market, text a few friends—all as if nothing has happened.

But secretly we are waiting.

If you have ever kept watch at the bedside of someone you love, you know that you will endure one long night in exchange for one more dawn. That is the bargain hope makes. And when morning comes, hope comes with it that the day will be better than the night before.

Every sunrise is a natural sign of hope. The farmer pauses in the routine of early morning feeding and wonders at the play of light on the fields. The fisherman makes a final check of his nets, weighs anchor, and fills his lungs with the incredibly pure ocean air. Even the factory worker on the midnight shift pauses amidst the machinery and stands tiptoe to look through the grit-encrusted windows to see if there is any light on the factory deck. If there is, soon it will be time to wash up; another night has passed.

The psalmist was undoubtedly thinking of the watchman stationed on the old Jerusalem wall who, as the night wears on, watches less and less for enemy invaders and more and more for morning relief. We don't know what distress had befallen the psalmist, but she confesses that she waits for the Lord to dawn in her life even more than that watchman waits for the morning. Then, as if to reinforce her anguish, the poet repeats the line: "I say, more than those who watch for the morning."

Genuine hope entails one of the least attractive activities known to impatient people: waiting. That little button in the elevator, *close door*, is there for people like us to punch impatiently. It's a placebo. The door will close in its own good time. Life will run its course. Our mantra is, "I've got to run." I've got to run because I'm on a treadmill of obligations with eternity to pay. A treadmill of worries about security, career, health, love, money, and death. And I'm afraid if I quit running the machine will continue and grind me into its gears. I want to stop but I am afraid.

In the Gospels Jesus's ministry, too, is portrayed as a rush from one good deed to the next, from one act of compassion to the next, many of which are introduced by the word "immediately."

But then he dies. And when he dies, something in the universe grinds to a halt. His friends lay him in a tomb and then, in honor of the Day of Rest, they leave him to God and walk away. And Jesus—his dead body, that is—waits, as it were, for something to happen.

When we commit a loved one to the elements, we commend the loved one to God. The word "commend" means to place into someone else's hands. We say,

> May God the Father who created this body,
> May God the Son who by his blood redeemed this body,
> May God the Holy Spirit who through baptism sanctified
>   this body—
> keep these remains until the day of the resurrection of all
>   flesh,

and then we do a funny thing. We walk away. But secretly we are humming the psalmist's tune.

Hope thrives in its natural habitat, which is distress. The best places to read (or sing) Psalm 130 are places of unhappiness. I have a colleague who calls this "dislocated" Bible reading. I would call it well located. Read about the resurrection in the cancer center at your local hospital or at an intake facility along the US–Mexican border or in an unemployment office. Read about it in a cemetery. Stand in the fresh dirt. Talk to the dirt. Say to the dirt, "Hope thou in God, for I shall yet praise him, who is the health of my countenance and my God."

Václav Havel reminds us, "Hope is definitely not the same thing as optimism. It is not the conviction that something will turn out well, but the certainty that something makes sense, no matter how it turns out." The King James Version quaintly translates Romans 5:5, "Hope does not disappoint," with "Hope maketh not ashamed." No matter what, I will not be ashamed of my hope. Why not? Because it doesn't expose something naïve or foolish in me, but witnesses to God's goodness. It reminds me that God's promise makes sense.

So, the question of hope is not the poor relation in the philosopher's trio of questions. For the Third Question is really the First Question. For if you are grounded in hope, you know more than you thought you did and with a different way of knowing and in a different spirit. And with hope in your heart, your ethics change. For hope is a way of living openly and generously toward others. The Christian struggle for justice is inconceivable apart from the hope that empowers it. Telling the truth is unthinkable apart from the hope that someone will hear it for what it is.

What may I hope? The question never gets old or goes out of style. You may hope in the God who raised Jesus from the dead! The resurrection is a pillar of fire illuminating the night sky, soaring ahead of the human journey. It is testimony. Not only to God's love but to God's justice. If you want to know where God stands on the issue of suffering or oppression, if you want to know what God thinks when he sees his children killing one another, if you want to know what God feels when he sees you walking away from a cemetery—go to the tomb of God's son. Go early. Wait patiently. Listen for testimony.

Some years ago, when Hurricane Fran visited our city, it damaged countless homes, destroyed thousands of trees, and knocked out power for a week. We were a city in the dark. When Sunday came around, a smallish congregation gathered for worship. Still without power and light, we were a devastated little group.

Our pastor had the good sense to introduce the service by inviting anyone who wished to do so to tell a hurricane story. Now, Lutherans do not do this. But after some appropriate display of reticence, we began. Some witnesses recounted rather trivial losses, like an air conditioning unit, a favorite tree, or a few shingles, but gradually the stories gave way to something deeper. It soon became clear that we had more than a hurricane on our minds. A woman testified of a cancer she had endured; another spoke of her divorce. An old man, who was not accustomed to making speeches in church (who is?), stood at his pew and there in the darkness recalled a terrible battle from World War II.

As Sunday mornings go, it was amazing.

The stories varied greatly from one another, and who could verify the accuracy of every detail? Most of them did not have happy endings, but each one mattered and made sense. Every one of the stories testified to some *side* of God's faithfulness. Each story seemed to say, *I waited on the Lord; so can you!* From that miscellany of stories, a shadowy figure began to emerge as if from a mist or a tomb: not one of the tellers but the Object of all our tales.

We are waiting for him now and for the light that only he can shed in our lives. We confess that we have more questions than answers, and more failings than we like to admit. But to the Third Question, which is now our First Question, we have an answer:

I wait for the Lord, and in his word do I hope.

12

THE PROMISE OF PENTECOST

"I will not leave you desolate."

—JOHN 14:15–20

What most of us know about Pentecost comes from its founding story in the second chapter of the book of Acts. As described there, it is a spectacular, if somewhat chaotic, event replete with tongues of flame and the sound of rushing wind. The Holy Spirit descends on the apostles, and they begin testifying in languages other than their own. This draws a crowd of Jewish pilgrims, and now each of them is hearing about God's "deeds of power" in his or her own language. This is a wonder.

But let's not go there. There is a prequel to all this excitement, and it's found in Jesus's Farewell Discourse, covering nearly four chapters in the Gospel of John. There we discover that Pentecost does not begin in excitement but in loneliness. And before it is miraculous testimony, it is a promise given in the dark.

It's a quieter, more subdued scene. Jesus is presiding over his last meal with his disciples. The air is heavy with a sense of doom. He has just given the morsel to Judas, identifying him as the one who will betray him, and Judas has bolted from the room to be swallowed by the night. Inside, imagine Jesus seated at the head of the table, his face illumined by candlelight. He is speaking to his friends with great solemnity and at some length. It is his Long Goodbye. Tomorrow he must die, and his friends will be alone.

Someone has said that the world lives by only a few great speeches, that is, by words spoken in the right place, to the right people, and at the right time. The world is filled with mistimed, misplaced speeches. We long for what the philosopher calls "right speech." One thinks of Lincoln's Second Inaugural at the close of the Civil War, or Martin Luther King at the Lincoln Memorial. The night before a crucifixion is not the time to say, "Everything will be all right." It's not the occasion for a lecture or the giving of a law. What is the right word for the Lord's last night?

It is a promise.

"I will ask the Father, and he will give you another Advocate, to be with you forever. This is the Spirit of Truth, whom the world cannot receive, because it neither sees him nor knows him. You know him, because he abides with you, and he will be in you. I will not leave you desolate. . . . On that day you will know that I am in my Father, and you in me, and I in you."

A promise can be given at any time. Your mother is ill, old, and worried. She is feeling alone. What will become of me? she asks. It falls to you to say, "Mom, we will always care for you, no matter what. I promise you." The child is afraid of the dark. And why shouldn't she be? There's a monster living under her bed. It falls to you to say, "There is not a monster under your bed. I promise you."

This is not the same as saying about a young artist, "She shows great promise." That means we already see the signs of greatness about her. No, the promises we need occur in the dark, in the absence of signs or evidences of success. In these situations, the promise is everything. There are no other grab bars. The promise is only as good as the one who makes it.

Our life in this church is rich with both kinds of promise. There are detectable signs of the Holy Spirit among us. How could we say otherwise as we gaze upon a table, laden with silver vessels brimming with God's gifts, the company of believers gathered around it? But "church" also happens where the indicators are not so hopeful.

Several years ago, the Diocese of North Carolina assigned a priest to initiate a ministry to the Latino community in the eastern part of the state where many were working in agriculture or the chicken-processing plants. How to begin? A feasibility study? An advertising blitz? Here's what he does: he takes a card table, a hand-woven blanket, and some bread and a cruet of wine to the local laundromat, and there he sets up shop. Within weeks, Pentecost happens and a congregation materializes. Soon the patrons are crossing themselves and waiting for a break in the Mass to switch their clothing from washers to dryers. The "Laundromat Priest," as he is known, intones the Great Thanksgiving during the spin cycle. A newspaper reports, "They stand respectfully toward the rear of the washerette, as if occupying holy ground."

About this church you could say, it doesn't have much promise. On the other hand, *all* it has is the promise (and it has proved to be more than enough): "I will not leave you desolate."

The whole world needs the promise of Pentecost, because desolation is everywhere. I read with interest that earlier this year the British government appointed a cabinet-level official to tackle the epidemic of loneliness in Great Britain. The minister of loneliness. Look at all the lonely people, another Brit sang, where *do* they all come from? First, we think of the elderly, but loneliness has many faces: the bullied, the closeted, the housebound, the mentally ill, the chronically ill, those with failing memories, the grieving, the incarcerated, and, of course, the *different*, who often find themselves alone in a crowd.

In our great cities millions of people live what the poet called "lives of quiet desperation." In New York City, an enterprising fellow has created a network of lonely strangers, now numbering in the thousands, who gather virtually on a weekly basis—to do what? To talk to one another. It is an intervention desperately needed. What were once interhuman transactions are routinely conducted impersonally between and among invisible strangers. Online banking, online education, online shopping—all such transactions have one thing in common: no one will occupy your life-space to smile at you and say, "It's good to be with you again. How've you been?"

Now it is also possible to go online and confess your sins and receive absolution. It works like this: first, select the appropriate sin from a drop-down menu of sins, then, after a few intermediate steps, click on Forgiveness, and you're done. No altar, no candles, no passing the peace, no off-key singing, no crying babies, no cold coffee in the narthex. Nothing of what we once meant by "community." Only you. The miracle is that your heart can select the proper response and be forgiven this way. But it is a lonelier way to go.

Consider the worst traffic jam you've ever seen. Think of it as a metaphor for what life has become for many. Millions of anonymous people trapped in their cars, cells, apartments, rooms, or hospital beds with no one to say, "I love you," or to inquire about their well-being. And at the end of life, a caring nurse, to be sure, but no one to anoint them with oil, to make the sign of the cross, or to speak a blessing.

In the darkness of *his* room, which is known to us as the Upper Room, Jesus has a vision of the profound loneliness on this our lonely planet. And so, he makes a promise that goes something like this: "I will send a Helper to cut through the occlusions and scar tissue of your world. I will make a way out of no way. I will send you a Helper who will open a channel through the loneliness of this life. He will make *me* available to *you*."

The many translations of that one little word, "helper"—*Paraclete*—that is, one who is called to the side of another, show how hard it is to define the Holy Spirit: advocate, helper, comforter, counselor, Spirit of Truth. Strange for a preacher to say, but it's hard to talk about the Holy Spirit because when it comes to divine things, we are all children, and children need pictures. But there are none. No pictures, only *effects*. Because of this, for many Christians the Holy Spirit remains the Unknown God.

The most common misconception of the Holy Spirit is that the Spirit's purpose is to give us more of *us*. As if the Spirit's job is to give me more of *me*, much in the way a five-hour energy drink provides a boost: Is your church small? The Spirit will make it big. Are you having trouble paying your bills? The Spirit will make you rich beyond your wildest dreams! Do you sometimes feel like a loser? Is the whole cosmos kicking sand in your face? The Spirit will make you a winner. Do you sometimes struggle in your faith, even entertain a doubt or two? The Spirit will erase your bad mind and fill you with boundless enthusiasm.

To be fair, toward the end of his letter to the Galatians, Paul *does* list some human behaviors that he associates with the Holy Spirit. But they aren't the muscular claims we hear so much about. They are accurate reflections of God's presence in our lives: love, joy, peace, patience, kindness, goodness, gentleness, and self-control.

Further, in writing to the Corinthians, Paul claims that no one can speak this three-word sentence apart from the Holy Spirit: "Jesus is Lord." Which means that we can't even share a word about Jesus or recite the Apostles' Creed without the Spirit's help. If this is true, how much more, then, is the Spirit needed outside the walls of the sanctuary? Who but the Holy Spirit is *helping* those who are trying to follow Jesus in supposedly "secular" venues—in cancer wards, classrooms, courtrooms, kitchens, shelters, jails, war zones, and refugee camps around the world? Who is it but the Holy Spirit who "sets the solitary into families"?

The Greek word for "desolate" is *orphanos*—from which we derive the English word "orphaned." About twenty-five years ago that translation came home to some of us in a moving way. It was a baptism performed very near to where I am standing. Some of you may remember it, as I do, for the tragic circumstances that surrounded it. The baptism of the child followed exactly one day after the funeral for the child's mother. Funeral on Saturday afternoon, baptism on Sunday morning. Never was the Holy Spirit more needed—or present—than in our church that day.

I also remember it for the sermon our pastor delivered. Pastor Prehn normally stood stolidly in the pulpit and preached from a manuscript. But on that morning something took hold of him, and of course we all knew what it was. With the child cradled in his

arms, and with tears in his eyes, he preached his sermon while walking—no, pacing—up and down, up and down, the center aisle of
the sanctuary. I don't remember the particulars of his message, but
I do remember what it was about. It was about promise making: the
promise the triune God was making to this child at her baptism, and
the promises we make to support and love one another. It was not
a perfect sermon, only the *right* sermon for us and for our time and
place. It seemed to me then, as it does all these years later, that Jesus
is *always* promising us, "I will not leave you *orphanos*."

"On that day you will know that I am in my Father, and you in
me, and I in you."

In the Gospel of John, *that day* is not judgment day or the last day
of history, but *today*. *That day* is the scary day in which we feel alone
and abandoned in the world. Who knows the hour? The doors of
our lives open onto *that day*. Each of us goes straight from this place
into the heart of *that day*.

On that day—*today*—"I will not leave you desolate."

Triumph

13

EMPIRE

He answered, "I tell you, if these were silent, the very stones would cry out."

—LUKE 19:28–46

The dean of the chapel has asked me to announce that this year's passion play will be much the same as last year's passion play. We have decided not to change the plot or substitute new characters. Once again, the followers of Jesus will hoist him onto the back of a donkey, spread their tunics on the cobblestone path, and accompany him into the capital. Once again, a good-sized crowd will surge into the street and, joining the disciples, the two groups will create a perfect storm of praise. As they did last year, the spectators will hail him as their messianic king.

From here, the plot will descend as usual. Once again, the falling action will be enough to break our hearts. The same people will tell the same lies. Judas will betray. Peter will deny. Pilate will cower. The Sanhedrin will not change its vote this year. On Friday, the play will end as it always does with the same insincere actors crying, "The King is dead," or something to that effect. It has been ordained.

Our lives are governed by dramatic rituals—weddings, funerals, birthdays, sporting events, pomp and circumstance at commencement, the family reunion at the lake with the same games, the same potato salad. There's no escaping the expected. Today, we stand at the gateway to the most sacred of all rituals: Holy Week. Holy Week is a dredging machine used to hollow out a great canal, and the canal is us. Every year it cuts a little deeper to the core of what it means to be a follower of Jesus. With each pass something in us is exposed—and healed. So, let there be a parade with liturgical dancers and palm branches and exuberant children—just like last year!

Since we know how this ritual ends—in death—why raise such a spectacle? Do we really need these dancers? Shouldn't these children be in Sunday school, where they can be seen but their hosannas not heard? Is all this joy necessary, really?

We do it this way because, if only for a moment, we want to see its true significance. We say our hosannas, stand in silence beneath the cross, grieve his death, and welcome him on Easter morning because we belong in this story. We are its actors, not spectators. We do it because we need to join the chorus: "At the name of Jesus, every knee shall bow / in heaven and earth and under the earth . . . / and every tongue confess that he is Lord."

On Palm Sunday the Lord entered Jerusalem to establish his empire. He entered the polis to claim what was his. It was a political act. You don't stage an entrance to the capital without political ramifications. One doesn't challenge the values of empire without proposing an alternative empire of your own.

We Christians often make a point of denying that Jesus came to establish an earthly kingdom. We are wise to say that because, if he had such designs, we wouldn't have known where to put him in our world. Where exactly does a king on a donkey fit amidst the empires, nations, and multinationals? Where does his message of peace fit in a world of spiraling violence, mass shootings, suicide bombers, and computerized warfare? Where does he fit in a world in which it is possible to launch an air strike on a house in Baghdad from a computer in Nebraska? Is it any wonder that on Palm Sunday and many other occasions besides we offer our hearts as the only refuge for this displaced king? Because that's the only place he fits.

But the Palm Sunday spectacle does not mention the heart. What all four Gospels *do* say is that he rode into the capital surrounded by followers who hailed him as a messianic king, and that the religious and civil authorities deemed him to be a serious enough threat that they had him killed.

He was not killed because he told harmless little stories about wheat fields and shepherds. Nor was he killed because he was good with children and urged his followers to become childlike. He was not killed because he said, "I want to be the king of your heart." He was killed because he spoke truth to power. Like the *Titanic* and the iceberg, two empires were colliding. He was not killed because he aspired to be the new Caesar but because he claimed to be Caesar's Lord.

He may have *said* his kingdom was not of this world, but the first thing he did when he entered a public place was to kick over some tables in the Exchange and perform an act of justice. His road took him from the highway of public acclaim through the labyrinthine corridors of power until it became a thorn-infested path only one man could walk. Like his entrance to the city, his crucifixion was an equally public affair, about which the apostle Paul would later say (to a king, no less), "This thing was not done in a corner."

More than fifty years ago the civil rights movement staged a march from Selma to Montgomery, the capital of Alabama. I say "staged" because the march, like Jesus's entrance to Jerusalem, was not logistically necessary. Both were symbolic, and both broke a fundamental rule: Thou shalt not rejoice in the face of oppression (because to do so implies that you are in touch with a *greater* source of power). Thou shalt not dance and clap your hands in the face of power. Thou shalt not sing in the face of your own fear. Thou shalt not tell the truth to those who don't want to hear it. You may remember that the march in Alabama ended with a young black minister standing on the steps of the state capitol and shouting, "Be jubilant, my feet! Our God is marching on!"

That's why the parade had to be stopped at all costs. Not because of what it was but because of what it symbolized. In the case of Selma, it signified an exodus from the bondage of segregation to political freedom. In Jesus's case, it signaled the entrance of the Prince of Peace into the kingdom of violence. If we allow this interloper on a donkey to challenge the rule and values of empire, what will happen to our world? What will happen to us? You know very well: he will change us.

In the documentary film *The Fog of War*, an eighty-six-year-old Robert McNamara reflects on the war in Vietnam in which 3.4 million people lost their lives. (As a young man, McNamara was also involved in planning the firebombing of Dresden.) He says, "The human race needs to think more about killing. . . . Is that what we [really] want in the twenty-first century?" It was good that the former secretary of defense had the character to rethink history and his own role in it, but his comments raise an obvious question: Who will save us from the mood swings of history? Who will save us from the acts of destruction that appear strategically necessary to one generation and hopelessly wrong to the next? Who will save us from the ritualistic round of apologies for the sins of previous generations? Is there some eternal standard to which we can look for guidance and hope? Yes, there is. Look at the spectacle unfolding before your eyes. Look at the man on the donkey. The prophet Isaiah saw him first:

> For every boot of the trampling warrior . . .
> Will be burned as fuel for the fire. . . .
> For unto us a son is given;
> And the government will be upon his shoulder
> . . . of the increase of his empire and of
> Peace there will be no end.

Palm Sunday promotes nothing less than joyful insubordination in the face of evil and death. This morning I am thinking of an old and dear friend. Her name was Linda. She had already done two rounds of chemotherapy and was about to begin the third, experimental course. She knew the terrain. She knew about the nausea and the fatigue. She knew how to prepare not for the unknown but for the all-too-well-known. Since she was a woman of faith, she had an idea. She rented a VFW hall, hired a band, and on the night before her treatments were to begin, she went dancing with her friends. I have never heard the gospel preached more joyously than it was danced that night by a bunch of arthritic Lutherans.

Which only goes to show you: the best dancing is done on the devil's dance floor.

So, we *must* have a parade on Palm Sunday. We must rejoice at the beginning of Passion Week. Not because we are in denial but because we are not afraid. Not because we underestimate the enemy but because love is stronger than death.

There is a language appropriate to what we feel. It is praise. I attended an exciting basketball game the other week, and I was so annoyed because the two guys sitting behind me talked about nothing but business throughout the game. Amazing things were happening on the court, but all I heard was talk of mergers, business models, and "optimization." There is a language appropriate to basketball, and it isn't "optimization." There is a language appropriate to concert performances that lift you off the ground. There is a language appropriate to love. And there is a language appropriate to standing in the presence of the King of Glory.

I wish I could say that praising God is good for your health. I'd like to report that researchers at a famous medical center have determined that those who praise their Lord live on average 1.7 years longer than those who don't, and that they enjoy a more robust quality of life. But all I can really say is that our praise *belongs* to him. It's like the woman who anointed him with expensive perfume whose fragrance filled the whole house. It's like the extravagance of his burial. On Friday he will be sealed in a tomb with a store of spices and ointments fit for an emperor. The cost-benefit ratio of adoration is always out of whack. But it's *Jesus.* The praise belongs to him.

The keepers of the status quo understand, and it scares them witless. That's why they tell you and me to be quiet. "Keep your witness inside the church. Don't stick your nose in where it doesn't belong, or you could lose your protected status. Keep it to yourself. Religion is a private affair between you and your own heart."

But Jesus says, "I tell you this, if these are silent, the very stones beneath this animal's hooves would cry 'Glory!'" If we are silent, the very marble that lines the corridors of power will shout, "Praise him!" The praise is as *necessary* to him as his suffering. It is unstoppable, and we belong to that Glory Train.

Dear friends, we face an agonizing week ahead: Rejoice!

14

IT IS FINISHED!

When Jesus had received the wine, he said, "It is finished."
—JOHN 19:28–30

You have probably noticed that modern medicine does not excel at endings. When a terrible illness begins to take its course, medical technology throws every weapon at its disposal into the fray. Standard treatments give way to new treatments, which spawn innovative treatments, which produce "the latest" therapy, after which lies the territory ahead—an ominous experimental therapy whose only name is a government number. Finally, when the end comes, we have no words with which to greet it. It's as if we have spent all our language on the future, and, in the face of death, we are dead broke. The wrap-up at the hospital is terse and ordinary. You leave a multistoried temple of medicine with a plastic bag of personal effects, and hope you can remember where you parked. Death is an anticlimax.

The literary critic Frank Kermode once said that narrative plots, and life itself, are like the *tick* and *tock* of a clock. We construct this rhythm because we need an identifiable beginning and a meaningful ending and something of significance in between. In fact, he said, it is only the *tock* that makes sense of the interval between beginning and end.

Does it seem curious to you that after all these years we are still preoccupied with the *tock* of Jesus's death—with each word and each detail of his ending? In the 2,200 pages of James Boswell's epic *Life of*

Samuel Johnson, the protagonist's death is dispensed with in 36 pages. In the Gospels, on the other hand, the circumstances of Jesus's death constitute between 50 and 60 *percent* of the narrative. The passion narrative is anything but an anticlimax. At the end we count out his last words as if they were silver dollars. It is as if the whole church presses its ear to the parched lips to hear the legacy. Our questions are like those of any grieving survivor in any hospital waiting room: *Did he suffer? What did he say? Did he mention me?*

The clinical answer to these questions is quite straightforward. He died more quickly than those who know about these things might have expected. During the six hours of his dying, he expressed the full range of human anguish—from the absence of water to the absence of God. He was kind to his mother and generous to his executioners. When he died, it was as if he was handing his life over to someone else. Oh yes, one last thing, at the very end he gave out a cry and said, "It is finished."

In the English language the word "finished" has two meanings. It can mean "completed": we finish a chair to bring out its beauty; well-to-do young women used to be sent to terrible places called finishing schools. When a neighbor finishes building his garage, he has something to show for it.

In Great Britain, it is otherwise. There they have a way of saying "finished" to mean the opposite, namely, that something is all gone. When you pass through a cafeteria line and ask for some kidney pie, the server behind the counter will say, "Sorry, luv, the kidney pie is finished." By which she doesn't mean it's complete and ready to eat, but that it's all gone. Not completed but depleted. *Deleted.*

When a family gathers round the bedside of one who has died, a silent debate is raging among the survivors. The widow wants to know, "Is my husband finished like a meal that has been consumed, or is he finished like a runner who has completed the course?"

Today, we say "completed." We trust that when Jesus cried out, "It is finished," he meant more than "The agony of my longest day is over." The Greek word John uses can be translated "completed."

Which is fitting, since in John's Gospel, unlike the other three, Jesus has absolute command of his own ending. In John's Gospel there is no weeping in the Garden of Gethsemane. No cry of forsakenness from the cross. Only in this gospel does Jesus say, "No one takes my life from me. I lay it down of my own accord."

"It is finished" does not exactly resonate with us. For if there is one thing missing in our environment, it's the sense of completion. Many are inclined to agree with the writer Franz Kafka, who said, "The meaning of life is that it stops." Like a clock or toothache. Our culture has lost an authoritative sense of ending. We find ourselves living in the arrhythmia of *tock-tick* time, caught between stories, seeking some greater significance for our lives, avoiding the ending at all costs.

Some are convinced that we don't need the definitive *tock* of completion. Look carefully and you can see it in the eyes of students and young people; it's the sparkle of an exciting adventure that lies just ahead or around the corner. Our culture doesn't have time for completion. We want to strive and grow and make and know *more*. As Saint Augustine said, the only thing that will satisfy human creatures is more and more being. We are on the make for *more*, and we simply don't have time to ask what it all means. The most boring word in the English language, and the one most out of place in a culture like ours, is "finished." If you think you're finished, well, my friend, maybe you *are*.

We hang upon Jesus's last words because, despite our protests to the contrary, there is nothing we want more than a life of wholeness. For although we have the need for *more* built into us, there is already something called *enough* that has been given to us. We are moving toward something we already *have*.

For those whose life (or death) fits no orderly pattern, Jesus's triumphant cry offers completion when we need it most: now. We need the fullness of "It is finished" to sustain us while we are still on the journey. Without Christ's triumphant cry, Good Friday is an absolute horror. It's an unraveling. A return to chaos and the void. Without it, your life and mine are nothing more than the turning of pages, one after another, with no plot, no theme, and no good ending.

When we were kids on the playground, we used to say, "Don't start a fight you can't finish." That was schoolyard bravado circa 1955. This is grown-up talk: Don't start a *life* you can't finish. Don't go careening from one godless thing to the next, like a bus without a driver, expecting that it will magically add up to something. Rather, invite Jesus to complete every plan and relationship along the way, just as long ago he finished what God had begun from eternity.

"Did Papa mention me before he died?" the ne'er-do-well in the family asks, as if his sorry life might be redeemed by the word of a dying man. "Tell me, did he say my name?"

To all of us who can't stop striving for *more*, Jesus's cry is the promise of peace. It is the Lord's final assessment of his life and ours.

Sure enough, he *did* mention you just before he died: he said you can stop running.

"It is finished."

15

Sermon Preached in an Empty Church

Then their eyes were opened, and they recognized him.

—LUKE 24:13–35

Today's lesson from the Gospel of Luke is a drama in three acts. Exactly how the resurrection of Jesus occurred we do not know. It is not pictured in the Bible. But we do know how it occurs among God's people. In the story of the supper at Emmaus, it occurs in three movements. They are Discouragement, Recognition, and Amazement. Those three acts correspond to the dramatic changes in our lives as well, and especially as we endure the hardships of COVID-19, or what our forefathers would have called the plague.

Act I. *Discouragement.* You can't experience discouragement unless first you have its prerequisite: hopes and dreams. We are all dreamers. We can't stop ourselves from constructing elaborate mental futures and scenarios. Our plans may include adventures, travel, family celebrations, a variety of successful outcomes, and, at last, financial security. We are always "just turning the corner" or "getting on our feet" or finally "making it." No one is too young to learn discouragement: "I was looking forward to graduation," a high school senior says (because she has already made a mental picture of it), "you know, when they play Pomp and Circumstance and we walk in in our robes and everybody's there." A grandchild laments, "We had hoped to see the Grand Canyon for the first time this June."

In all this there is more than disappointment. Just beneath the children's dream is a grown-up fear, fear that the life we have loved will change beyond our ability to embrace and enjoy it. It is not just the Grand Canyon. It is something bigger than the Grand Canyon.

This morning we meet two of Jesus's followers who understand our situation more profoundly than we understand it ourselves. When we first meet them, they are headed the wrong way on the Yellow Brick Road—away from the Emerald City. They are taking the road that leads away from the epicenter of their religion, Jerusalem, away from their focus of holiness, Jesus. They are walking away from their own dream.

On the road they meet a stranger who appears to be ignorant of all that has happened in Jerusalem. There is nothing more maddening than someone who doesn't know enough to be discouraged. Who doesn't understand the gravity of the moment. So, the two disciples take it upon themselves to educate this stranger on the topic of discouragement. The verbs they use tell us a great deal about their state of mind. They say, "We had hoped that he was the one to redeem Israel." *We had hoped.* In grammar school they taught us "grammar"— that the past perfect tense, or pluperfect, denotes an action that has been completed in the past. Once we had a hope, but it is no more. You thought hope was about the future, but in this case it is about the past. They recall that some women went to the tomb and couldn't find his body. They even saw a vision of angels. But back to our topic: we *had* hoped.

Suddenly the stranger who seems so uninformed at the beginning of this conversation, who appears to know nothing about discouragement, takes over the conversation and becomes the teacher. And what a marvelous teacher he is. He is so filled with everything they lack, especially knowledge and hope, that they ask him to stay with them.

In our moment of discouragement, we say to this same stranger, "Stay with us, our day is far spent. We ourselves are far spent. We want only to be in your presence. We do not ask for a miracle, only You. The Very You. No need to take us up on a mountaintop. Nor even into a fine church with stained-glass windows and marble and expensive linens on the altar. Just come into our homes, sit with us at our kitchen table, and have a cup of coffee. Our kitchen is nothing special. But You can make it so."

Act II. *Recognition*. In London's National Gallery there is a painting by the Renaissance artist Michelangelo Caravaggio. It is called *The Supper at Emmaus*. Whenever I visit this museum, which isn't very often, the *Supper* is the first place I go to stand and watch. The painting does not depict a fancy dinner but an ordinary meal. Only four characters are portrayed in it: two disciples seated at either end of the table, the stranger in the center, and a server standing at the side. One of the things I love about the painting is that the fourth side of the table is open to the viewer. It is our place at the table. You can stand there and watch, or you can join the meal.

The stranger is blessing the bread. And as he does so, we are given to observe the precise moment of recognition. One disciple's arm is flying toward the viewer as if to penetrate the invisible wall between the figures in the painting and us, the viewers. The other is caught coming off his chair in utter amazement.

It is the recognition scene, when the gauzy veil between us and the Divine is suddenly ripped apart. It happens many times in the Gospels: when "doubting" Thomas places his hand in Christ's wound and cries, "My Lord and my God!" It happens in the dark on Easter morning when Mary Magdalene mistakes the risen Christ for the groundskeeper. All the shadowy figure needs to say is "Mary," and she replies with an inflection we can only imagine, "Teacher," in a voice that says, "More Than Teacher."

Our recognition scene occurs in the breaking of the bread when we, though many and now separated from one another, receive the meal that makes us one. But it occurs in other moments as well—like now, for example, in this historic moment of pandemic, when just as we were about to say, "*We had hoped*," we, too, recognize him at our table.

Act III. *Amazement*. If the great Caravaggio was right, when recognition occurs, amazement is not far behind. "That very hour," the disciples make a U-turn on the road and start walking—I think running—toward their future. They are heading back to another meeting with Jesus in Jerusalem. Once again, he will suddenly appear, and there will be more fear, then amazement. It is not a ghost. He is risen.

This morning when I came into this church to preach, my heart sank. The place was as empty as a tomb. Just me and the video recorder. Over the years I have dreamed up many a sermon, almost always alone. I have even preached them alone in my kitchen or out behind the garage. But I have never *delivered* one in an empty church. It is strange.

But isn't this the triumph of resurrection? He is not a prisoner in this sanctuary. We cannot hold him here in this beautiful building any more than he could be held by Joseph's impressive tomb. He is out and about and on his way to Galilee with other things to do.

Of course, we can "see" him by faith in the breaking of the bread, but also in hospitals, laboratories, schools, grocery stores, nursing homes, funeral homes, banks, buses, and trains, wherever the friends of God are expending themselves on our behalf.

It is a mystery, and I cannot explain it: after Jesus was raised from the dead, he was hard to recognize. He ate and drank and, as Caravaggio pointedly demonstrates, cast a definite shadow on the wall behind him. But even those who, like us, had followed him for years failed to recognize him in the garden, on the beach, or on the road.

Something about resurrection frees him to appear in other guises; to move into new identities and to embody others with his love. The Jesuit poet Gerard Manly Hopkins, wrote, "for Christ plays in ten thousand places, / Lovely in limbs, and lovely in eyes not his / To the Father through the features of men's faces."

Now I can "see" him roaming the corridors of nursing homes, like someone making rounds, pausing to bless those who are alone and in distress. Perhaps he's the young man who pushes the gurney, every day exposing himself to death in order to help others. Or he might be the overwhelmed chaplain, who had been considering retirement, but now finds herself, prayer book in hand, alone in a dreary crematorium except for God and one of God's lost children.

Is there any amazement left in us when we recognize such courage? Can there be any greater amazement in the presence of such love?

Jesus once appeared as the Stranger, veiled even from the eyes of those who loved him. He is still here. Disguised. Incognito. I wonder if he is wearing a mask these days. It would be just like him.

Then their eyes were opened, and they recognized him.

16

GOD HAS GONE UP WITH A SHOUT!

When he had said this, as they were watching, he was lifted up, and a cloud took him out of their sight.

—ACTS 1:6–11; PSALM 47:5

We say it every Sunday, not because we understand it, but because it's in the script: "He ascended into heaven and is seated at the right hand of the Father." He ascended. The idea behind reciting a creed is reasonably simple. If you do not say the right words, you may not be in the right story. For example, if you don't hear the lines "To be or not to be, that is the question," chances are you are not watching a performance of *Hamlet*. The script will tell you that.

The story of the ascension follows a familiar pattern in Luke's script. We might call it the divine escape. It begins early in the gospel. After his first sermon in Nazareth, Jesus is taken by his parishioners to the edge of a cliff, where they plan to push him off, but he passes through them, and Luke says he "went away." Later, on the Mount of Transfiguration, a cloud overshadows him, and the scene appears to be set for yet another escape. But when he could have gone away, he instead chooses to descend the mountain and head toward the cross. At Emmaus, after he opens the Scripture and blesses the bread, he disappears. Finally, at Bethany, he preaches to his followers essentially the same sermon he had preached in the synagogue at Nazareth, about fulfilling everything written in the law, the prophets, and the psalms. Then he fades from the scene. This time he is really *gone*. As he blessed them, Luke says, "he parted from them."

The end.

I recently watched a documentary on the making of the famous antinuclear movie *Dr. Strangelove*. Apparently, the filming went well until the end. The problem was, no one knew how to end the movie. So, they filmed three endings, and the director, Stanley Kubrick, simply picked one, and it stopped. It *is* a problem. How do you escape a fantasy world in such a way that the audience can leave the theater and resume their lives?

Luke faced a similar problem. He had no idea his first book would be such a hit. As any successful author might do, he produced a sequel. As with any sequel, a little overlap is inevitable and perhaps desirable. In volume 1, the Gospel of Luke, the ascending Jesus is the living *End*. His disappearance represents the triumphant, Hollywood-style end of a life in which nothing further can take place. In volume 2, the Acts of the Apostles, the ascending Jesus is the *beginning* of an exciting movement, one that will see its share of triumphs, to be sure, but also persecution, internal conflicts, suffering, and many tattered endings. But the *ascending*—the ascending is so important that it serves as the linchpin that connects two scripts: the life of Jesus and the mission of his followers.

Yet the ascension is oddly missing from most celebrations of Jesus. In the second congregation I served, we observed Ascension Day every year with a choral concert and an ice-cream social. I never preached on those occasions, preferring to let the music and the ice cream convey the message. Like most pastors, I was only grateful that Jesus had ascended on a Thursday and not a Sunday, which meant that I never had to make sense of the picture of Jesus ascending into the heavens as he triumphantly ends one ministry in the flesh and begins another in the spirit.

But if you wish to make sense of death, then you must reckon with the ascension. For death and the hope of triumph are written in *our* script too. When we say, "He ascended into heaven," we are saying as much about ourselves as we are about God.

We read stories about death every day. Death's script appears often unexpectedly as the lead story but more predictably in the obituaries.

If you are a habitual reader of the obits, you'll notice that, lately, the obituaries have changed. In the past the obituaries in our local newspaper were strictly boilerplate. Each was written with the same tone of factual objectivity, as if the most exciting news about a person's life was his or her place of birth, degrees attained, or Masonic affiliation. But now the obits have become interesting, because our newspaper has invited surviving friends and relatives to write spiritual accounts of their loved ones' lives.

The parents of a boy named Ray write that Ray has graduated from middle school to a higher form of knowledge. Another says a chap named Wallace has moved up to a higher stage of development. Most of the obituary writers, however, use traditional religious language: George has fought the good fight, kept the faith, and therefore a crown of righteousness awaits him. Bessie has loved the Lord her whole life and has now gone home to be with Jesus.

It is about time the newspapers allow us to tell the world what our lives really mean. How much imagination does it take to absorb the brutal facts and conditions that attend a young woman dying of cancer, a child struck by an automobile, an old man breathing his last in a nursing home? Is this all there is to report?

Those of you who have attended the dying—and the dead—have entered fully into the chaos and finality of the event. Then, at the very end, when all you are left with is a corpse and a tableau of grief, you have absorbed the scene into your soul and reframed it. You have *added* something. Depending on your tradition, you have made the sign of the cross upon the forehead, eyes, and breast; you have anointed the body with oil, recited a psalm, made a blessing, said a prayer. You have added something, which is a way of saying, "There is more to this story than meets the eye."

Fifty years ago, Martin Luther King Jr. was murdered in a seedy Memphis motel. He bled to death on the balcony with one leg protruding through the rail at an awkward angle as his friends wept and dabbed at his wounds. May none of us meet such an ending.

Today, when you walk into the undercroft of King's first church in Montgomery, Alabama, the first thing you see is a startling piece of religious art. It is a mural depicting a life-sized Martin Luther King in a cream-colored robe and cincture, arms extended in bene- diction, as he ascends into the clouds surrounded by the mothers and fathers of the African American church. They are on their way to heaven. If you've seen the photographs from the Lorraine Motel, you have every right to ask which is the true ending of Martin Luther King—the scene on the balcony or the scene in the mural.

Which is the true end of each of our lives? Most of us conclude our lives in the descendant rather than the ascendant mode. You might have witnessed a loved one's end of life in an emergency room or on the freeway. You think you have caught sight of your own mortal end, and you do not like what you see, because not only does it not look pretty, it doesn't look finished, and certainly not triumphant.

But no. The script says more. It says, "He ascended." And when you make that confession, you are speaking of your own destiny as well. He ascended: he moved onto his own higher plane. He graduated. He fought the good fight. He went home.

Some preachers read the ascension as a prelude to modern humanity's sense of alienation in a world from which God has departed. But the church has chosen another lens, that of Psalm 47, through which to read the event, and it is not forlorn or tragic but triumphant:

> God is gone up with a shout!
> the LORD with the sound of a trumpet.

The ascension marks Jesus's entry into heaven. When I was a boy, I loved the poem by Vachel Lindsay about the founder of the Salvation Army, titled "General William Booth Enters into Heaven." Except I always imagined that he was not speaking of General Booth but of Jesus. Let me substitute the name Jesus for Booth:

Jesus led boldly with his big bass drum.
        Are you washed in the blood of the Lamb?
    The Saints smiled gravely, and they said, "He's come."
        Are you washed in the blood of the Lamb?

I suppose it would be too much to expect the church to celebrate Christ's triumph as boisterously as it deserves and to let it go at
that. But Christians have long made a *problem* of the ascension. They
have debated the exact *location* of the heaven to which he ascended.
Where exactly does he sit at the right hand of God? In what place?
Martin Luther sweeps all the cards off the table with his interpretation: "The right hand of God is everywhere." Jesus had to leave
one place so he could be *everywhere* in heaven and earth so that his
fullness could fill all in all.

We stand between two advents, the first and second coming of
the Lord. That means that we are free to look for Jesus in all the
wrong places, for he is coming toward us from more than one direc-
tion. He might not be coming from Bethlehem anymore, but from
the Mount of Ascension as our triumphant Lord. *Everywhere* means
that the one in whom we hope is not always receding into the murky
past (as all things strictly historical must) but is waiting to meet up
with our confessions of faith wherever we are. Our job is not to re-
trieve Jesus from history but to *meet* him where he promised to be:
among those who suffer and seek redemption, in the neighborhoods,
hospitals, cemeteries, and lost causes where the risen one is coming
into the world.

A few Easters ago my wife and I were driving through eastern
North Carolina at twilight, through some of the most depressed communities in our state. We passed a cottage where someone had taken a
piece of poster board and made a little sign and planted it at the end of
the driveway where everybody on the main road would have to see it.
Written in magic marker, it said, "The grave could not hold him."

It was roadside poetry at its best. Almost conspiratorial, like a
revolutionary slogan. "Psst. The grave could not hold him. Pass it

on." Because he is risen and now ascended, he rules. The Lord is now free to be "everywhere."

Every story in the Bible has what might be called a performance response. An expectation. Something it wants you to *do*. For example, when Jesus says, "Go, tell your friends what great things God has done for you," it's not hard to guess the appropriate response. Every text suggests an action: to do, think, strive, give, grow, love.

For those who believe they control their own destiny, the story of the ascension demands the most difficult response imaginable: wait. Wait for the Spirit to be poured out. Wait for God to come into your lives. Go to Jerusalem, get a room, and wait. They are to wait for the Holy Spirit. And even though the Holy Spirit has been given to the church, the command to wait has not been rescinded. When a congregation or an individual has lost the power to wait, spiritual death is sure to follow. It will be a death marked by enormous outlays of activity, to be sure, but death it will be. Only those with a risen and ascended Lord can wait. For he comes to us, not we to him.

> Because he comes to us in the final descent, at the loose
>   and fraying ends of life,
> wait for him.
>   Because his victory belongs to our script,
> wait for him.
>   Because there is more to our stories than the brutal
>   facts,
> wait for him.
>   Because the grave could not hold him . . .

17

I Saw Satan Fall

The seventy returned with joy, saying, "Lord, even the de-
mons are subject to us in your name!" And he said to them,
"I saw Satan fall like lightning from heaven."

—LUKE 10:1–21

In the last congregation I served, a small group within the church set aside every Monday evening for witnessing in the community. Since we were Lutherans, we gave this practice an innovative, cutting-edge kind of name. We called it Evangelism Night. It worked something like this. Around 7 p.m. the callers would come into the church kitchen, drink coffee, pray, and go out in teams to visit people who were unchurched, new to the church, or mad at the church. Along about 9:15 the teams would start dribbling back for more coffee and the sharing of stories. There were stories of families still "shopping" for a church home, stories of lonely people, stories of angry people who had forgotten why they were angry, stories of sad and searching people. Nothing spectacular.

I miss Evangelism Night, not so much for the stunning success stories, since "success" was not a prominent part of our vocabulary, but for our growing sense that we were participating in a pattern of ministry that was older and larger than ourselves and not of our own devising.

Luke has uncovered such a pattern in this Gospel lesson. It is the pattern of calling→sending→witnessing→returning. Luke didn't invent the pattern. Jesus didn't invent the pattern either. It begins with God, who tells Moses early on, "Go tell them 'I Am' has sent you. I will be with you." It's as old as God's conversation with Isaiah: "Whom shall we send, and who will go for us?" And the prophet's reply: "Here am I, send me." It was God's way with Jesus, who was sent on a dangerous mission and murdered in the course of it, and who returned to the Father in triumph. It is Jesus's way with the church: "As my Father has sent me, even so send I you." Calling→sending→witnessing→returning. The pattern persists.

It's the *return* part of the pattern that interests me the most: "The seventy returned with joy, saying, 'Lord, even the demons are subject to us in your name.' And he said to them: 'I saw Satan fall like lightning from heaven.'"

This is a powerful mission text, known as the Sending of the Seventy, which is found only in the Gospel of Luke. It must have been a galvanizing text for the surging Christian movement. It's reflected in Jesus's parting message to his disciples in the book of Acts: "You will be my witnesses in Jerusalem, in all Judea and Samaria, and to the ends of the earth." But even the most cursory comparison of the early church's mission to the gentiles and our own evangelism efforts reveals a significant difference. They were poised like commandos about to make a raid on a pagan society. A mission situation like theirs can be diagrammed on a blackboard, with the *x*'s standing for the missionaries and the *o*'s representing the objectives.

I was once a member of a mission congregation, and I must admit our program was not that clear-cut. In retrospect, it seems we were susceptible to what might be called "beachhead theology." We had as our objective the establishment of a base camp in our own neighborhood, from which we would launch reconnaissance patrols into other neighborhoods further afield. In these various operations, however, we met few genuine pagans. Rarely, if ever, did we encounter one of our neighbors bowing before a statue or sacrificing a chicken. Even those who didn't attend church claimed to be "born again," or at least had the odor of affiliation about them. Our little church was making an assault on a society that already considered itself Christian, whose public schools observed the Christian holidays, whose judges opened court with prayer, and whose leading politicians regularly accused one another of (gasp!) "not being a Christian."

We had grown fond of describing the church as a countercultural community, but that seemed more a wish than a reality. Instead of a diagram of separation, our situation resembled an amoeba-like circle in which we were included rather than excluded. The amoeba was called religion, and almost everyone we met had their share of it.

We had trouble seeing clear-cut lines, but without them, it was hard to get ready for battle. And with no battle, no victory. And with no victory, no joy.

In the Sending of the Seventy, what looks like a modest evangelism program provokes in Jesus a stunning non sequitur. The returning apostles say, in effect, "We did well." He says, "I saw Satan fall like lightning from heaven!"

I am thinking of a street preacher in our city. I can see him. He stands in the median of a four-lane road, bullhorning his vision as motorists hurriedly raise their windows and turn up their music. "I saw Satan fall" is his cry. This preacher is not interested in the survival of the church. He's not a man for pews, pulpits, or committee reports. He's not about strategies, objectives, or ten-year plans. He is watching something taking place on the rim of eternity. He sees souls attempting to escape the burning pit of hell; he sees the glow of paradise beckoning to everyone on that highway. God has entrusted him with a vision that will change us forever.

In our text, the gentle Galilean storyteller named Jesus has been replaced by an apocalyptic preacher whose eyes are on fire with eternity. He sees things no one else sees. It's as if he has infrared vision. He sees the birth of a new age in which people who were excluded from the original plan of salvation are now being embraced.

In the book of Genesis, seventy is the number of the earth's nations after the flood. "Seventy" is all of us. Jesus not only understands the symbolism of seventy, he is practicing it in new ways. In

Jesus's ministry the kingdom is breaking out of the circle, outside the amoeba, and moving toward tax collectors, prostitutes, sinners, and "foreigners." "This fellow welcomes sinners and eats with them," say his perceptive critics. The church's move into gentile territory does not simply represent the extension of the organization, like adding a few more Starbucks franchises. It signals a change of age in which the Lord is claiming us all as beloved children. That's where Satan is being defeated—not in the comfort zones of our world but on its margins.

We see something small: he sees something big.

We see churches struggling for solvency: he sees a larger and more exciting arena in which God's power is at work.

We see improvements here and there: he sees a transformation under way fueled by the Holy Spirit.

We see the church at its most fragile: he sees the church at its most majestic.

In *The Screwtape Letters*, C. S. Lewis gives us a series of unforgettable messages from a senior devil named Screwtape to his nephew Wormwood. Wormwood, as many of you know, is down on earth (or up on earth, if you will), trying to tempt people away from the Enemy—God. Screwtape tells his nephew, "You want your patient to quit God? Show him the church." He continues, "I do not mean the church as we see her, spread out through all time and space and rooted in eternity, terrible as an army with banners. That, I confess, is a spectacle which makes our boldest tempters uneasy." No, he says, take him to a local church. "Make his mind flit to and fro between an expression like 'the body of Christ' and the actual faces in the next pew."

Look at the church. Jesus sees things we don't see, makes connections we don't make, except perhaps on those occasions like Evangelism Night, or in a moment of reconciliation between old enemies, or in a Eucharist in a hospital room. At such moments the *pattern* of what God is really doing in our life together becomes blessedly clear.

When Jesus says, "I saw Satan fall," he poses a challenge to our eyesight. For he is seeing a reality that is far thicker than anything our senses or sciences can measure. Even people who don't believe in anything remotely *like* Satan will pause and say, "Really? Where? When?"

On the seventh night of rioting and protests over the killing of a black man by a white policeman, and with American cities everywhere aflame, I saw Satan fall in Fayetteville, North Carolina. It happened when sixty police officers in riot gear knelt on the pavement before an angry, oncoming crowd. Stunned and tearful, the two lines mingled into one.

Lightning from heaven in a southern town.

The school where I teach offers classes at several North Carolina prisons. By definition, a prison is a restrictive place, and a warden must run a tight ship. At the entrance to Women's Prison in Raleigh, a long list of rules is posted on the wall. They are absolutes. Many of the rules forbid what we would consider normal human behavior, such as friendship, small favors, or personal conversations. As our course was concluding, one of the students who had served ten years was about to be released. Her crime had been considerable. She was a Christian. We requested that she be allowed to attend the year-end communion service in the divinity school chapel. Since she was soon to be released anyway, the request was granted. The warden was good enough to accompany her in the prison van. This was a generous gesture, but most surprisingly, she was permitted to participate in the Eucharist as a server. With three hundred people singing "Just as I Am, without One Plea," and with tears in her eyes, she helped distribute the bread.

And the warden received the body of Christ from an inmate.

Nothing spectacular, you might say. Certainly, not reported on CNN. Only a slight wrinkle in the order of things. Just another excursion into God's kingdom. But I saw a possibility I had never witnessed in a prison or a church. It's something our beloved Lord, the Street Preacher, sees every day—and celebrates. It is the ultimate triumph of God over the forces that hold our planet in bondage.

Let's ask him again to tell us what he sees, and maybe if we're lucky we'll see it too: "I saw Satan fall like lightning from heaven!"

The Life of Faith

18

JUST TELL THE TRUTH

*"And I myself have seen and have testified that this is the
Son of God."*

—JOHN 1:29–34

Last week the three wise men were snowed in. They made it as far
as the Washington Duke Hotel for brunch but couldn't make it to
church. Just when we needed the Epiphany in the worst possible way,
it was canceled.

An "epiphany" is usually associated with something good, like
an unexpected act of courage from a coward or a generous gift from
a tightwad. A glimmer of hope in dire circumstances can qualify as
an epiphany.

In Christian terms, the best epiphanies derive from the great
Epiphany of God in Jesus Christ. It happened when one of the Eastern sages looked up from his astrolabe and exclaimed, "My God,
look at that star!" It occurred when John the Baptist recognized his
cousin and cried, "Behold, the Lamb of God." The early church celebrated Epiphany long before it observed Christmas, reasoning that
the Lord's *appearing* was more important to us than his quiet entry
into the world.

Today is the eighty-eighth birthday of another sort of epiphany.
His name was Martin Luther King. Like John the Baptist, he too
testified to something greater than himself and, like John, paid the
price for it. Today is also a farewell of sorts. For with this Gospel

reading, we say good-bye to John the Baptist until he returns in Advent as a voice crying in the wilderness. But before he begins his long hibernation, John comes to us on this special day with one last request.

He wants us to tell the truth.

Just tell the truth is an uncomplicated request in a very complicated world of untruth, half-truths, counterfactuals, alternate truth, fake news, and disinformation. It is a world in which language has been weaponized and *lying* has become a geopolitical weapon. The new Oxford dictionary has chosen "post-truth" as its word of the year. To cite an example or two, we have been told that 9/11 and the horrific events associated with it were a false-flag event orchestrated by the American government. That Barack Obama was born in Africa and ineligible to serve as president of the United States. That the massacre of children at the Sandy Hook School in Connecticut was fabricated in a plot to discredit the gun industry. The children were actors. It never happened.

Of course, we don't believe the lies, but their persistence and cruelty eventually sap the spirit and wear us down. They are morally depressing, as only big lies can be. They can evoke two responses in us. We can remain perpetually knotted in anger toward forces beyond our control, or we can withdraw from the public world and tend our personal gardens. The first option is bad for us, the second is bad for the community.

One hundred years ago, the poet William Butler Yeats wrote "The Second Coming," a poem that prophetically captures the moral chaos of our day. It contains these lines:

> Things fall apart; the centre cannot hold;
> Mere anarchy is loosed upon the world,
> The blood-dimmed tide is loosed, and everywhere
> The ceremony of innocence is drowned;
> The best lack all conviction, while the worst
> Are full of passionate intensity.

It's hard to believe that there was ever a time when one person could appear in the wilderness of Judea (or on the streets of Selma) and tell the truth with such clarity and power that, even now, we would give anything to hear that voice again. Or that a man named Jesus would offer so much love that we are still held together by it, even when things seem to be falling apart.

In the face of disintegrating circumstances, the Gospel of John demands an honest witness to the truth. His gospel is the most poetic of the four, yet, paradoxically, more than any other, it reads like a legal document. It reads like a trial transcript set into poetry. Of John the Baptist it says, "He was not the light. He came as a witness to testify to the light." The next section is introduced, "This is the testimony of John." Whether it's Nicodemus interviewing Jesus by night, the woman at the well plying him with questions, the man born blind being grilled by the Pharisees, a servant girl quizzing Simon Peter, or Pontius Pilate cross-examining his prisoner, the interrogations never stop. *Who are you? Where is he from? Who made you well? Are you a king?*

John the Baptist has put us on the stand, and there's no pleading the Fifth. The biggest lie of all is the whopper we've been telling ourselves for too long, namely, that witnessing to Jesus violates the individual rights of others. Besides, we don't need to testify because American values are "more or less" Christian anyway.

That is the Serpent talking.

The great Catholic peace activist Dorothy Day once said, "If I have achieved anything in my life, it is because I wasn't embarrassed to talk about God." She was not ashamed to make the connection between feeding the poor or opposing war and the revelation of God in Jesus Christ. Or, as Martin Luther King often replied when asked why he opposed the war in Vietnam, "Before I became a civil rights leader, I was a preacher of the gospel."

Why do we Christians find it difficult to express our deepest convictions? I can give you an account of my academic training and the development of my thinking on a variety of subjects. I can explain in passionate detail my various sports allegiances. I can tell you the cities

I've lived in and the jobs I've held in chronological order. But stop me short and ask where I stand on the role of Jesus in American life, and I may hem and haw about the separation of church and state and worry about offending someone. The Bible says, "Always be ready to make your defense to anyone who demands an account of the hope that is in you." The deepening divisions in this country are God's way of getting us *ready*.

John the Baptist says, "I have come to bear witness to the truth." It seems everyone in the Fourth Gospel talks about truth: John, Jesus, even Pontius Pilate. But in the information age "truth" has become passé. In fact, the first casualty of the information age *is* truth. Consider, for example, Jesus's words, "Ye shall know the truth, and the truth shall make you free." You can find this sentence inscribed on the walls of many churches, but also above the entrance to the CIA headquarters in Langley, Virginia.

What is truth?

Americans have been stumped by Pilate's question for a long time. So long, in fact, that a type of cynicism has developed among professing Christians. Cynicism says, "If I believe in certain religious dogmas, such as the divinity of Jesus and the superiority of Christianity above other religions, I can support any political option." It was Martin Luther (not Rev. King) who once said, mistakenly, "Jesus Christ has nothing to do with politics." If 2016 postelection statistics are accurate, the majority of white American Christians agreed with him by voting against their own religious instincts.

Scripture teaches that God takes the side of those who are being overburdened by the rich and powerful. Next to idolatry, God's care for the poor, the widow, the orphan, and the alien is the favorite topic of the Old Testament prophets. The poor have become a part of God's name—the God *who* delivers the poor.

How is that name honored in the halls of power? In our state it is illegal for any municipality, no matter how rich, to raise the minimum wage, effectively legislating poverty for thousands. Our chosen politicians systematically work to deny health care to the poorest of the poor. You can see the great company of the uninsured in emergency rooms around the state, where they sleep on the floor, with their families, or in wheelchairs waiting all night for routine health care. How can we square such scenes of avoidable desperation with the ministry of Jesus or the prophet's question—and answer: "What does the Lord require of you? To act justly, and to love mercy and to walk humbly with your God."

It goes without saying that Jesus is not a Republican or a Democrat (there, I said it), but he does have a platform, and it's been published! We know it as the New Testament. His platform does not support the idolatry of power, nor does it feed on self-aggrandizement. The religion of the cross is not about winning. It begins with sacrificial love—Christ's love for us and for all people. It includes welcoming the stranger, caring for the sick, forgiving enemies, forgoing violence, upholding life, and glorifying God in all that we do. The planks in his platform do not represent optional lifestyle choices for Christians. They are the hallmarks of those who claim his name.

A few days from now, a powerful man will place his left hand on a Bible and swear to preserve, protect, and defend the Constitution of the United States. If he follows precedent, he will seal his promise with an oath to God. It will be a transfixing moment in modern American history. All the turmoil of the past year and the hope for the future will be caught in the crosshairs of that defining moment. I hope and pray that just as the new president takes his oath, Christians everywhere will lay a hand on the Scripture or make the sign of the cross on our hearts and remember that we too have testimony to give. Not just in relation to one president or one administration, but for the rest of our lives.

"Do I have a witness?" Jesus asks.

Yes, it is your people.

What Dr. King offered us fifty years ago was nothing complicated or hard to understand. He wasn't a politician. He was a Christian language teacher, and the language he taught us was basic Christian testimony. In a few powerful strokes, he taught us how to do justice and to temper it with the love of mercy. And in so doing, he told us who we are as a people. To those of us who resisted (and there were and are many), he told us who we might become.

When I was a kid, my mother always told me what your mothers told you: "As long as you tell the truth, you won't get in trouble." Our mothers lied. "Did you cause your brother's nose to bleed?" "Yes, I did." "It's good that you told the truth. You're not in trouble, dear, but you are grounded for three weeks."

You see, it's just the opposite: Tell the truth, and that's when the trouble starts.

Tell someone in the statehouse or in Washington about justice and mercy, and I'll wager you'll wind up in somebody's database. It finally caught up with John in a big way when he told Herod that, on balance, it is not a good idea to sleep with your brother's wife. It cost him his head. It's what happened to Jesus when he finally got fed up with Pilate's philosophizing and told him the unvarnished truth.

It's not often acknowledged that, late in his career, Martin Luther King took a sabbatical from talking about brotherhood. Instead, he started preaching about racism, a word he rarely used in his younger days. Then he came out against the war in Vietnam, for which every civil rights organization except his own and every news outlet in America, including the *New York Times*, denounced him.

He was left alone on the narrow ledge of testimony. Shortly before his death, they told him to quit marching. He replied by testifying:

> I don't march because I like it;
> I march because I must.
> And because I'm a man
> And because I am a child of God.

Just tell the truth. That's when the trouble starts. I can't know the shape of your trouble.

I don't know what the cost of your discipleship will be. But I do know this: John told the truth. Martin told the truth. And so can we.

19

ACKNOWLEDGMENT

He answered, "I do not know whether he is a sinner. One thing I do know, that though I was blind, now I see."

—JOHN 9:1–41

Jesus is adhering to an ancient and mysterious standard of care when he mixes dust and spit into a sticky paste, then places it on the man's eyelids and kneads his eyes. He "anointed" them, the text says. We don't know if he prayed or uttered an incantation as he did so: "Light of the world, Light of the world." He sends him to a pool called Sent, *Siloam* in Hebrew, so named because its waters are figuratively sent by aqueduct from the mountains above to the pool below. The man goes to the pool and begins bathing dead tissue that has never registered a sunset or the olive-colored eyes of a woman, eyes that have never recognized. Dead from birth. And something happens.

He first sees light. Then his own reflection in the pool of Siloam. Then a fantastic tapestry of colors in the narrow, crowded streets of a Middle Eastern marketplace. He sees the geometrical shapes of buildings, the green and brown of olive trees, the purple and yellow of exotic fabrics being sold in the stalls; blue sky and puffy white clouds. Only later does he see the face of the one who healed him. Only later does he see the light.

In that instant he probably forgot how he had been a lifelong object of theological speculation. I'm sure Jesus's disciples were not the first to toss a nickel into his cup, thinking that their act of generosity entitled them to speculate out loud concerning the causes of his mis-fortune. "Rabbi, who sinned?" This man has been afflicted from birth. If we assume that all afflictions are caused by sin, it follows that either this man sinned *in utero* or his parents sinned before his birth.

This is fake logic, and Jesus rejects it. The alternative is not an explanation but an authoritative work—followed by a good story.

What the poor man doesn't realize is that now, as a sighted per-son, he will continue to be the object of a different sort of specula-tion. The *cause* of blindness—that is theologically interesting. But the *cure* of blindness! That is a matter of life and death. For now you are making a decision about Jesus, about the one who only days earlier stood in the temple courtyard, (perhaps) as they lit the great torches, and cried out like a demented god, "I am the light of the world!" We had better get to the bottom of this, the authorities said.

In this story the cure itself takes exactly two verses. The contro-versy surrounding the cure, thirty-nine verses. And that is the rest of the story.

The rest of the story is that good people know sin when they see it but don't always acknowledge the power of God, especially when it occurs outside our accustomed channels. When this man returned to his community healed and praising God, one would have thought the religious leaders would have rejoiced with him. I would have expected the neighbors to fall on his neck with kisses, as if he were a returning hero. Why indeed not?

In the last church I served, one of the pillars of the congre-gation stopped by my office one morning to tell me he'd been "born again."

"What?" I said.

"Yep, last week I visited my brother-in-law's church—they call it a 'tabernacle'—and I don't know what it was, but something hap-pened, and I am born again," he said with irritating jubilation.

"You can't be born again," I said. "You are a Lutheran! You are a Norwegian! You are the chairman of the board of trustees." He was brimming with joy, but I was sulking. Why? Spiritual renewal is okay so long as it occurs within a familiar framework, and, most of all, so long as it doesn't threaten my understanding of God.

The novel *Revelation* by Peggy Payne is the story of a Presbyterian minister who has a revelation in Chapel Hill, North Carolina. One afternoon while grilling steaks in the backyard of the manse, he hears the voice of God speaking to him. It's a revelation. It's the kind of revelation that will change his life; he will never be the same. The rest of the story tells of the price he pays for revelation. Do the leaders of his congregation rejoice with him? Not exactly. They do provide free psychiatric care and paid administrative leave.

You can imagine how we would react if our minister were to announce that she had been the recipient of a direct revelation. The church could not contain such a thing. After appropriate counseling, she would be reassigned to development or some other administrative post away from the pulpit. We would do deep background investigations, recheck her transcripts, reread her references, but eventually she would have to go for claiming to see things to which we are blind.

It's not difficult to sympathize with the Pharisees. They are only attempting what many of us have been trained to do: to observe, describe, and explain the phenomena. To that end, they conduct three ill-fated field interviews.

First, the neighbors aren't much help. They won't even claim the blind man as a neighbor. Some say it is he, but others say no, he didn't have that mustache. The fact is, they don't know him because they don't want to know him. He was never more than a piece of village furniture to them.

Second, the Pharisees' interview with the man's parents is an even greater disaster, for mom and dad have long since learned not to stick their necks out for this cheeky child. So, beyond the basic data, they only suggest, Ask him. He is of age.

Finally, the authorities perform a stress interview on the blind man himself. This also turns out to be a fiasco because the man deftly redirects the conversation and begins interviewing *them*, toying with them like a cat with a mouse. "Would you too like to be his disciples?" he asks mischievously. "Perhaps you would like a tract or a marked New Testament."

Yes, we can sympathize with the Pharisees. Haven't you ever listened to the testimony of someone who has just returned from Lourdes or Tulsa healed of gout or arthritis, who's thrown the crutches away, and—admit it—haven't you wanted to ask some questions or do a follow-up study? Have you never felt a twinge of doubt when all those glamorous but corrupt celebrities—courtesans and congressmen—whose sins are so much more interesting than yours, manage to get born again just as their scandals are cresting in the media? Where does all this religion come from?

The question of origins pervades the Gospel of John. In desperation, the authorities sink to the oldest of debate tactics: Poison the well. Assail the source of your opponent's argument. About the man named Jesus they ask, *Where is he from?* What rabbinical school did he attend? Where did he learn to break God's law? The formerly blind man is ready for them: "Where is he *from?* Why, this man restored my sight. Never since the world began has a man blind from birth received his sight, and you want to know where he's from!" Looking skyward, he continues, "He's from the north, *far* north. He is from the Father in heaven!'

Things have gotten out of hand by this time because the formerly blind man is experiencing the freedom of one who sees no longer from a human perspective but from God's perspective. Does this story mean that you must possess special knowledge to be a Christian? Must you see the way God sees?

No, not knowledge but *acknowledgment.*

The formerly blind man doesn't know all the correct religious phrases with which to interpret his salvation. He is not pious in the traditional sense or even respectful of his elders. What he knows for sure is that once upon a time he sat in the darkness and dust waiting to die, and now the whole world is drenched in sunlight. And he acknowledges that.

One thing I know . . . He might have said, "I don't have all the jargon about Jesus down pat like you preachers. I may never speak in high-sounding phrases about *Gawd* and the meaning of life, and I may be a little rough around the edges when it comes to dealing with my betters. But one thing I do know . . ."

And as he makes his witness to us, we realize that the man blind from birth has a multitude of sons and daughters with their own stories to tell:

One thing I know, one of you might say: back in September when I was a thousand miles from home and drowning in loneliness, I somehow got through that, and I think that Somehow was God.

One thing I know, another says: when I was going through my divorce, I hurt so much I couldn't sleep or eat and was so filled with hate I couldn't think, but somehow I endured that, and I know that Somehow was God.

One thing I know, another might say: I was getting blind every weekend, and my weekends began on Wednesday. But one day I looked in the mirror and saw myself for what I really was. That loser in the mirror was Jesus calling me to something better.

One thing I know . . . Isn't that a marvelous understatement? As if the only, teensy little thing you happen to know is—who saved your life!

No, you don't start with special knowledge but with *acknowledgment*. Perhaps not with a public profession of faith but with a prayer from the depth of need. You may say, "God, I am not sure how to name you, but I am sure I need you. I can't talk about you easily, as others do. I don't even claim to love you. But I acknowledge you and my dependence on you."

You must be careful, keep your bases covered, and beware of overcommitting. But God *is* going to get you. For in the end the Lord will break through your defenses with such a gift of light that it will dazzle your darkness and give you real vision.

Such seeing has two consequences. One is suffering, the other is joy. Both.

In the story, the formerly blind man pays a terrible price for his vision. He is kicked out of the synagogue, cut off from religion, Torah,
family, the sweet-smelling incense of the Sabbath, the certitude of the
law—all because he looked deeply and directly into the Light. The
world will take on new beauty, but not without a twinge of nostalgia
for what has been given up.

The second consequence is joy. The sort of joy that is born of
freedom. We are free from having to be religious experts or self-
appointed saints, free from having to calculate the cost-benefit ratio
of every decision we make, free to be brave in the world. We even
have the freedom to stand up in a god-free culture where so many
claim to know so much and to say, "One thing *I* know . . . and it is
no small thing. It saved my life!"

And to think, it all began with the visionary witness of a blind
man.

20

BORN AGAIN

"How can anyone be born after having grown old?"

—JOHN 3:1–17

One of my colleagues has a cartoon from the *New Yorker* taped to his door. It shows a distinguished-looking person in cap and gown about to deliver a commencement address. With a self-congratulatory nod, he says, "I hardly know where to begin. I know so much." This may be Nicodemus's problem. It's not that he can't conceive of being transformed by a new idea. It's just that it's been so long since he's heard a genuinely new idea that he's forgotten how to get carried away. He is trying to reposition himself spiritually, hoping to figure things out, trying to find himself, which is a bit awkward for him because he is a grown-up. He's supposed to have found himself a long time ago. Besides, he is "a teacher of Israel," and academics do not change their minds abruptly.

I suspect that's why he comes by night to interview Jesus. When you're young, you can say to anyone who will listen, "Oh, man, I'm lost. I don't get it. I am nowhere." When you are older and successful, that's not what people want to hear. The famous ballplayer-evangelist Billy Sunday was said to have walked out of a Chicago bar one day and said to his teammates, "I'm through. I am going to Jesus Christ." That almost never happens in a seminar.

When you are a man or woman of the world, you don't fall at the feet of Jesus and cling to the hem of his garment. You *confer* with

Jesus. You don't accost him in the quad or a public place, but you interview him in a bar at midnight where the music is loud and no one will hear your dumb questions. And when you finally get up your courage to speak to him, you will talk about God as if God were a theory rather than your heavenly Father. I'm explaining this to the younger people in the audience, so you will know how to keep your guard up when Jesus interviews *you*.

The beautiful thing about Jesus is that he will play this game for a long time. He will meet you in the shadows whenever you're ready. Any time, your place or his. He will listen patiently to the strangest questions. But eventually the game ends.

For whoever comes to Jesus always leaves with more than he or she bargained for. Nicodemus doesn't ask how to get into the kingdom of God. As far is he is concerned, he's already a good candidate for the kingdom. He wouldn't be here if he and his fellow rabbi, Jesus, weren't already members. He just wants a civilized discussion. Instead, Jesus tells him how to get saved.

Jesus says you must be born again. And here it gets a little complicated. (This is where you need a divinity professor at the helm.) The Greek word for "again" can also be translated "from above." You must be born from above. In the context of John's Gospel, it makes more sense to translate the phrase "from above," for in this gospel Jesus is the light that shines in the darkness.

It is precisely because Jesus is from above that people like us who live below are constantly misunderstanding him. It's one of the trademarks of the Gospel of John: everybody misunderstands Jesus. My favorite example is the Samaritan woman at the well who, when Jesus says, "I will give the living waters of eternal life," replies, "Wait, let me get my bucket." Not that we don't make the same mistake. Jesus says, "I have come that you might have life and have it more abundantly," and we immediately refer to our bank accounts or portfolios.

Anyway, Jesus says, "born from above," and Nicodemus hears "born again" and asks, "You mean I must reenter my mother's womb and pass through the birth canal a second time?" Mercifully, the gospel does not record Jesus's facial expression in this conversation. Before we are too critical of Nicodemus, however, let's admit he's onto something. In a classically influenced culture like his (or in a spiritual atmosphere like ours), anyone can be born from above. Anyone can "get in touch" with the source of light or espouse higher principles. It's relatively painless. But to be born again, well, that will require more pain and a miracle of the Holy Spirit.

So it is that Nicodemus becomes one of the biggest and most reluctant newborns on record. His stature, age, and religious accomplishments are such that for him another birth will be a terrible trauma, an event mixed with pain and blinding new perceptions. He will do what most babies do, which is to squint against the light and weep with nostalgia for the womb, the old country, the former life.

Soon Nicodemus will disappear from the conversation. It may be that he is too big, too old, and too much in control of his own affairs to subject himself to that trauma. As he slips into the shadows, his last words are a question: "How can this be?"

Today, we have no shortage of books attempting to answer Nicodemus's question. *How to Be Born Again* and similar titles appear on religious best-seller lists, but they sound to me like *Lessons on How to Enjoy the Beach*. Get it? It's a joke. There *are* no lessons on how to enjoy the beach—you simply inhale the sea air, listen to the rhythm of the waves breaking on the shore, and let the wind kiss your face. It's not a technique one can master. If you could master it, it wouldn't be the wind and the beach. Nor the Spirit.

Like all creatures, we have no choice but to submit to the wind. Who is to say whether this chance encounter or that tumorous growth, this melody in a café or that crushing defeat are merely the winds of chance that blow through everyone's life, or the signs of the Spirit's presence? What language shall we borrow with which to interpret our lives? For some it will be the formulas of spiritual certainty formatted as "laws," for others the evocation of mystery. But for both, a new birth.

Jesus's dialogue with Nicodemus preserves a space for mystery, a sacred vestibule to experience, decision, and language. The two rabbis speak under the cloak of darkness, and Jesus says that whatever happens to Nicodemus will resemble the breezes on a warm Judean evening. That's the way the Holy Spirit stirs in us too, even before we have words to name the stirring.

It will be a mystery, like the unpremeditated move from walking to dancing.

As Nicodemus fades from the scene, Jesus takes over the conversation. He says, "For God so loved the world that he gave his only begotten son, that whoever believes in him should not perish but have everlasting life." Here you don't need a "teacher of Israel" (or a divinity professor) to tell you what that means, only two ears and an open heart. God loved and God gave. The greatest pain of rebirth belongs to the Mother, to God. As the nurse said to my wife during her first delivery, "It *must* hurt." At the very heart of the universe is a Creator who is willing to hurt for all created beings in order to make them whole. God creates salvation by the mysterious instrument of God's own suffering.

Jesus calls it eternal life. Those who receive it cannot pretend to master their own spiritual health. God gives it to children in the waters of baptism, as well as to others who do not or cannot understand the magnitude of the gift. It's given to those who look at the stars and are moved to call upon him, and to sinners like us who look in the mirror and don't like what we see. In Jesus's day it was the social outcasts who had no other option than to ask him for a new life and a new start. Today, it's the young people who haven't perfected the self-protective measures their mothers and fathers have mastered, who haven't learned to keep their guard up, who aren't embarrassed to admit that they are looking for something better.

It almost sounds as if the one category of human being Jesus can't touch is people like me. People who can endlessly balance one idea against another, who are clever enough to defer the claims of truth indefinitely. I would like to ask Nicodemus about this myself. I would like to interview him. Of course, we would meet after hours in some leather-lined alcove on campus or maybe in a friend's law office—professional to professional, professor to professor—and I would ask, "Nicodemus, how is it with your soul, man? Did it ever happen for you? Did you find that eternal life you were looking for?"

But Nicodemus isn't talking. He is giving no more interviews. I can only tell you this about him: When Jesus was crucified, a man named Joseph of Arimathea claimed his body. When he came for it, he brought a friend with him, a man named Nicodemus, identified only as "the one who had come to him by night." Nicodemus brought with him one hundred pounds of myrrh and aloes and sweet-smelling ointments. Together, the two men laid him to rest in a garden tomb.

Once again, Nicodemus is meeting Jesus in the shadows as night is falling. This time with a change of strategy: not to quiz him but to anoint him. The two men perform the burial ritual in silence, which is another form of worship.

So, I put it to you: Was Nicodemus too old, too smart, too successful to catch the wind of the Holy Spirit? Was he born again? We're never told.

You can draw your own conclusions.

21

COUNTERSTORY

*He said, "Who are you?" And she answered, "I am Ruth,
your servant; spread your cloak over your servant, for you
are next of kin."*

—RUTH 1–4

Today's Old Testament reading from the book of Ruth takes us far
away from our sophisticated world of sex and political intrigue to
another, far simpler world of sex and political intrigue. One never
knows how many people are actually listening when the lessons are
read, but if you were concentrating on the reading from the book
of Ruth, it may have piqued your interest. It's not every passage in
Scripture in which one character advises another, "Fix yourself up,
put on your best perfume, and when he's had plenty to drink lie
down at his feet and wait for something to happen." Who said the
Bible is a dull book?

The book of Ruth is a Hebrew short story from which our lectionary reading provides little more than a few sentences. It would
be as if we selected several sentences from the middle of an Alice
Munro short story, and then tried to understand the whole story on
their basis. What's going on?

There's a Jewish woman named Naomi and her husband, Elime-
lech. They have two sons. And they are starving in Israel. So, they
leave their hometown of Bethlehem and migrate to the land of Moab
to the south. Things are better in Moab. The boys grow up and marry

"foreign" women, Moabites. One is named Orpah (that's not Oprah but Orpah), and the other is named Ruth. Then, in a stunning reversal of fortune, all three men die—first Naomi's husband and ten years later her sons, the husbands of Orpah and Ruth. By chapter 1, verse 5, the tally reads as follows: three men dead, three widows, and no children.

To make matters worse, these women live in a man's world. To own land, you have to be a man; to work the land and build a shelter, you need several men. To sustain your dead husband's name and to produce that most essential of social commodities, male babies, you need a man to impregnate you. To give you physical protection from the wrong kind of men, you need a good man, and, God knows, a good man is hard to find.

Naomi announces her intention to return home to her own people in Bethlehem. She firmly tells her daughters-in-law, "You are Moabites. Your future is in Moab. Besides," she adds bitterly, "I have no more male babies in my womb for you to marry. Stay in Moab."

I realize that I may be the only person who came to church this morning with a burning desire to know what ever happened to the Moabites. What most of us know, if we know anything about this short story, is Ruth's famous reply to her mother-in-law:

> Where you go, I will go;
>> where you lodge, I will lodge;
> your people shall be my people,
>> and your God my God.
> Where you die, I will die. . . .
> May the LORD do thus and so to me, . . .
> if even death parts me from you!

We know these words, of course, because they are often recited at weddings by the bride and groom, blissfully unaware that they are pledging eternal allegiance to their respective mothers-in-law.

So Orpah remains in Moab, but Ruth, like Abraham before her,

sets out with Naomi for the promised land of Israel. When they return to Bethlehem, they are greeted by a chorus of village women
who will provide commentary throughout the story, like the chorus
in a Greek tragedy. Naomi says to the women, don't call me Naomi
anymore, which means "sweetness." Call me Mara, which means
"bitter."

The two women arrive in time for the barley harvest. Naomi
sends Ruth out to glean in a field owned by a distant relative of hers,
an older, prosperous, and respected man named Boaz. Boaz notices a
new woman in the field and shows her a few gentlemanly kindnesses.
He makes sure she has extra water to drink, and he orders the young
men in the fields not to molest her, not to "touch" her, as Hebrew
puts it tastefully. He also orders them to pull some handfuls of barley
from their sheaves so she will find plenty to glean.

Ruth returns to Naomi in the evening, and Naomi, ever the
matchmaker, says, "I know this man Boaz. He is a good man. He
can redeem our family."

Then she hatches a plan worthy of Dolly Levi: When Boaz is
winnowing on the threshing floor tonight, she says, perfume yourself,
put on your best clothes, but keep your face covered. When he has
drunk his wine and lies down for the night, go to him. "Uncover his
feet, lie down, and he will tell you what to do."

It's precisely here at this climactic moment, as these two relative
strangers are about to begin what one scholar calls "an ambiguous
encounter in the night," that our puritanical lectionary cuts the story.
What happened?

We're not sure. We're not sure because Hebrew poetry is so tricky
when it comes to sex. The word "feet," for example (as in "uncover
his feet"), does not always mean "feet" in Hebrew. What happens,
though, is surprisingly honorable.

Ruth stealthily uncovers Boaz's feet and lies down. In the middle
of the night, the text says, Boaz awakens with a startle—perhaps he
was cold or sensed the perfumed presence of another. In any event,
the Hebrew says, he was "trembling." Boaz asks, "Who are you?" Out

of the darkness and the fragrant warmth of new-mown hay comes the voice of a woman very much in charge: "I am Ruth. Spread your wings over me, for you are next of kin." ("Wings," by the way, is another one of those words we're not sure about.) But did you catch the reversal? Naomi had said, he will tell *you* what to do. But instead, Ruth tells *him* what to do. She instructs him on his moral and religious duty. In effect, she says, "Marry me, stranger."

Boaz is an older man and, like a lot of older men, very grateful for the attention. He acts the gentleman, pronounces a blessing on Ruth, thanks her for not choosing a younger man—and suggests that she leave before it gets light.

When the day comes, Boaz, no longer trembling, goes to the village gate, which is an all-male establishment, and announces his intention to redeem a parcel of land that once belonged to Naomi's husband, to redeem the family, and oh, yes, by the way, "since it's my duty," he adds, "I might as well marry the young Moabite Ruth."

The story ends like the Shakespearean comedy *All's Well That Ends Well*. Boaz and Ruth have a baby—surprise, it's a boy!—and the chorus of Bethlehem women gather around Naomi celebrating the baby, but even more the faithfulness of Ruth. Their last words of dialogue remind Naomi that her Moabite daughter-in-law is more valuable to her than seven sons.

Now, what about the politics in this story? As the old preacher used to say, the sting of this story is in its tale. The story ends with a genealogy. The women called the boy Obed. Boaz was the father of Obed, Obed was the father of Jesse. And Jesse was the father of David, the king.

I have called the book of Ruth a short story, but it's more accurate to call it a *counterstory*. It reminds us that the stories we think rule the world are always being rewritten by another story. In a male-dominated culture, the bond of friendship between two women changes the world. In a Bible that's as patriarchal a book as you could find, we discover, tucked away, just after the book of Judges, the story of a strong woman whose every action is chronicled by a chorus of women. When the woman finally encounters the powerful man, we discover that he rules by day but trembles at night.

The little story of Ruth also challenges any nation's or church's xenophobia—the fear of the foreigner. We build walls and erect gates to protect us from outsiders. Who are they? The Hispanic sojourners who glean in our barley fields; the severely handicapped, so noticeably absent from our social events; gay Christians who are knocking on the door of ordained ministry in so many denominations—these are but a few of the strangers at our gate. But the church is not a gated community.

Later in its history, when Israel returned from exile, its leaders were obsessed with the purity of the community, so much so that they declared that all Jewish men were to divorce their foreign wives. But the little book of Ruth witnesses against this law and Israel itself by reminding its readers that the greatest of all the kings, David, had some Moabite blood flowing in his veins.

What *did* happen to the Moabites? (A good question; I'm glad you asked.) We have had a week of "what ifs": What if one of the candidates had carried one more state? What if another candidate had campaigned a little more vigorously? What if we had known then what we know now? These are the hanging chads of history. Let me add one more: What if Ruth had stayed in Moab—no king David and no son of David named Jesus (who also had a little Moabite blood in him).

The story reminds us that God has a vested interest in politics. He once chose a nation and a king and once subjected his own son to the political and the judicial process. But the book of Ruth portrays a God who achieves his political purposes in a hidden way. We know that God is capable of parting seas, speaking from Sinai, and launching the odd lightning bolt. But in the book of Ruth, God never shows up. Oh, the characters talk about God, the way we do, and invoke his name from time to time, but the old world of sex and politics keeps on turning just as it still does without God's spectacular intervention.

Does this mean that God is AWOL? No, God works through the courage of a young woman and the kindness of strangers. Most history books tell the stories of kings, generals, and presidents. As they say, history is written by the winners. Even in the Bible, Ramses, David, Solomon, and Herod receive a disproportionate amount of coverage. But in the book of Ruth God works from the inside of history—under the covers, as it were—prompting ordinary people to use their native wit and moral intelligence to help one another survive. God, absent? God was there in the darkness of Bethlehem crouching in the hay on the threshing room floor. And God was there in the same sort of darkness, in Bethlehem no less, crouching in the straw of a lowly manger. As the theologian Karl Barth said, "God is so unassuming in the world."

We have been conditioned to want much more than this unassuming God wills to offer. Some of you might have come to this school because your parents or someone in your family wanted you to learn how to live the grand narrative of power or influence. That's the story we all want for ourselves and, and if not ourselves, our children. "You could grow up to be president," we tell our first graders as we strap the book bag on their backs and begin to worry about their SAT scores. Some of us know of no other master story than the narrative of social or economic dominance. The university is a factory for such stories.

What the God of Ruth offers is a counterstory. A white woman in a Native American church was giving me a tour through her church in Robeson County, where African Americans, whites, Native Americans, and Hispanics all try somehow to live together. It's the poorest county in North Carolina. As we walked, she told me the terrible story of how her Lumbee Indian husband and two of her sisters were killed in an automobile wreck. There she was, like Ruth (she really said), a white woman living in an Indian community. She walked me over to an art glass window near the baptismal font. It was a memorial to her husband and her sisters. It portrayed two hands of slightly different hues clasped beneath a cross.

"Don't you see?" she asked. "This is the story of us all. When I married my husband, everybody warned me against a mixed marriage. A white woman and an Indian? Never. They said it couldn't work. I would never be accepted. But this church made us one. See, it's right there in the window."

I would give anything to make Ruth, Boaz, Naomi, and the women of Bethlehem come alive for you. Because in the realm of God, these characters are not dead. They live on in the moral and religious imagination of people like you and me who are looking for a better story in a world filled with lies.

Then, if I were to ask the question, "What ever happened to the Moabites?" you would reply, "We're here."

22

THE STRAIGHTEST ANSWER

"You are the Christ, the Son of the living God."
—MATTHEW 16:13–19

"That's a complicated question," my garage mechanic replied when I asked him exactly how much a new exhaust system would cost. "So much depends on other people," my contractor said to me when I asked him if I would ever move into the house he was building. "There's really no good answer to your question," our doctor replied when I asked him how long my dying mother would live.

"It could be on the exam," the professor says, "or not."

O for a straight answer. To anything. Is there a straight answer in the house?

You ask your child, "What time do you plan to be home tonight?" She looks deep into your eyes and says, "Susan's parents allow her to stay out till midnight."

I once asked a troubled friend of mine, "So, how is your marriage going?" "All our friends are getting divorced," he said sadly.

Is there a straight answer in the house?

Every year on the eighteenth of January the church catholic celebrates the confession of Peter, who in a riveting moment in Caesarea Philippi gave a straight answer. "You are the Christ, the Son of the living God."

In Caesarea Philippi no less, a city rife with gods, goddesses, and houses of worship. Archaeologists have discovered no fewer than

fourteen temples to Baal within its precincts. It was also the legend-
ary birthplace of the god of nature, Pan. Dominating the city was
a magnificent marble temple dedicated to the godhead of Caesar
Augustus. Caesarea Philippi—not a good place in which to ask, "Is
that your final answer?"

Now, we are not celebrating straight answers per se. Because we
know that sometimes the most definitive, authoritative affirmations
are dead wrong: "CNN declares Al Gore the winner in the state of
Florida." Martin Luther King used to say about white supremacists,
who were militantly certain of their beliefs, "Take genuine sincerity
and compress it into a small, closed space and you have the most
dangerous force in the world."

Peter speaks up. He gets it right, and even he gets it wrong. When
Jesus asks him, "But who do you say that I am?" he could have stalled
or asked for clarification. "What do you mean by the question? What
are its hidden assumptions?" But no, he says it straight. But when
this Christ, or Messiah, whom he has just confessed, begins making
ominous references to suffering and crucifixion, he gets it wrong.
"God forbid," Peter says. "This shall never happen to you." And in
the space of five heartbreaking verses, he goes from Peter the Rock
to Peter the Blockhead or, worse, Satan.

It's hard to get it right because even when you get it right you can
always get it wrong. Take the name Jesus Christ, for example. How
we long to hear that name spoken meaningfully in a pluralistic culture. Why must the absence of "Jesus Christ" be normative on CNN
and in most major news outlets? Among politicians, why must "God"
be a placeholder for whatever qualifies as the national interest or the
speaker's political advantage?

And yet, living as we do in what Flannery O'Connor called "the
Christ-haunted" South, it's also possible to hear the name bandied
about a little too routinely. When I see Jesus on a bumper sticker or
hear his name associated with a used-car dealership or a successful
football game, I'd rather not hear it at all. I'd rather go back to Dietrich Bonhoeffer's theology of the hidden discipline. Writing from

his Nazi prison cell, Bonhoeffer foretold a day when our grandchildren will move the world with the word of God. "It will be a new language," he wrote, "perhaps quite non-religious, but liberating and redeeming—as was Jesus's language; it will shock people and yet overcome them by its power; it will be the language of a new righteousness." At least Bonhoeffer understood that it costs something every time you say, "You are the Christ, the Son of the living God." Just as it cost God something to confess our names at Calvary.

By a happy coincidence, the day of Peter's confession falls only three days after Martin Luther King's birthday. There was a man who was not afraid to name the name in dangerous company and understood the cost of doing so. About preaching he said, "The vocation to speak is a vocation to agony." Of the cross he said, "The cross is not a piece of pretty jewelry. It's something you die on." We should not allow King's many accomplishments to overshadow the spiritual encouragement he gives to people like you and me, who in less dangerous circumstances must also name the name and get it right.

When I was a seminary student, everyone more or less dreaded preaching class, especially the first day of class. Because that was the day our venerable professor would, as was his custom, give a lecturette called "the foundational principles of the gospel." That part of the class was okay. A little slow, but okay. But then, having explained the gospel, he would begin pacing about the room, moving ominously toward the students, who by this time were desperately trying to avoid eye contact with him. We knew what was coming. At last his gaze would fall on one hapless student and he would say, "Now, Mr. Smith, stand up and tell us the gospel." And right there on the spot, if your name was "Smith"—no matter what your mood or your level of unreadiness—you had to rise and essentially confess your faith. He thought it was a good start for preaching. He thought it was a good start for life.

Ecumenists have known for a long time that the best place to begin interreligious dialogue is not shared values or common works of social improvement. As liberal theologian Harvey Cox noted long ago, genuine dialogue starts with Jesus Christ. Whose son is he? What do you think of him? How does your opinion of him shape your actions in the world?

The Latin word is *confessio*, which originally meant to speak together, as we do today. You may have noticed that Father Lawrence and I are concelebrating the Eucharist, an Episcopalian and a Lutheran. No big deal, except that for 450 years our two communions have forbidden it. But today, on the day of Epiphany, Lutherans and Episcopalians officially end hundreds of years of separation and confess our full communion in sacrament and ministry.

This is not a corporate merger like Time Warner and AOL but a corporate confession. It is a joining of voices. It is our way of saying that when Peter spoke up at Caesarea Philippi, he was speaking for us, too. But this is not our final answer. For even our straightest, most definitive answer is also tinged with hope in something as yet unseen and unheard. For we also believe that someday our little confession will join with others in a chorus of beautiful harmonies until the whole faithful world is singing as one, "You are the Christ, the Son of the living God."

23

CRISIS MANAGEMENT

*"And the master commended the dishonest manager be-
cause he had acted shrewdly."*

—LUKE 16:1–13

Today's lesson is brought to us courtesy of the business school rather
than the divinity school. About this parable John Dominic Crossan once remarked, "We're not sure what it means, but we know
we don't like it." Many of the parables of Jesus seem odd. This is the
only one that feels sleazy. Whenever Jesus associates the kingdom of
God—however obliquely—with a shady character like a hypocritical
judge, a slaveholding master, or a dishonest manager, it makes us
uneasy. The manager, or steward, as he is traditionally named, has
been charging exorbitant prices and skimming a commission off the
top. When he is abruptly fired, he quickly reduces his own profit
margin, recovers his boss's principal, and manages to scratch a few
backs along the way. See, everybody wins! He is on a moral holiday
and invites us to tag along.

Like everyone who reads this parable, we are initially filled with
distaste at his amoral behavior, then moved to something closer to
admiration. Because, let's face it, we kind of *like* him. We can't help
ourselves. He is the rogue we publicly despise but secretly admire,
who somehow manages to game the system and land on his feet. The
Teflon Steward. We like him because the parable *makes* us like him by
showcasing his cunning while hiding his victims from our eyes. Jesus

refers to him twice as "unjust," but in some translations he is called the Shrewd Manager, a title that indicates some measure of admiration.

The Shrewd Manager is a projection of that part of ourselves we keep hidden. He gets away with things we would never try. We play it safe; he plays it fast and loose. We play by the rules; he bends them with ease. We can relate to the white-collar type who is "too weak to dig and ashamed to beg." He is the entrepreneur who peddles his worthless start-up, the hacker who busts the big boys, then testifies in exchange for immunity, gets a great book deal, and wows them on *Late Night*.

Despite our secret admiration, we are confident that the Lord will join our better selves in repudiating everything he stands for. If it's true that every parable delivers a shock, this is ours: "and *the* (not 'his' as in the NRSV) master commended the dishonest manager because he had acted shrewdly." What's more, the Greek word for "master" can refer either to the character in the story or to its Teller, Jesus.

Either way, how could "the master" commend such a rogue?

Most readers instinctively think of parables as guidelines for living. If the manager is commended, does it follow that we should "go and do likewise"? But what is it about the manager we should imitate? I confess that I have preached this parable so many ways that it makes my head spin. Mostly, I have followed the church's great interpreters, like Luther and Wesley, who have treated the story as an *example* story that gives Christians permission to exercise a little shrewdness, to wheel and deal, for only the right causes (of course).

We may criticize the theology of some of the religious celebrities among us, but secretly we admire the skill with which they promote themselves, sell their books, build their wealth, and take charge of the National Prayer Breakfast. "If only we could do that," we muse, "for the right reasons, of course." We salivate over shrewd Christian entrepreneurs who put together "deals" in order to build TV ministries and orphanages in foreign lands. Shouldn't we be like that too? (Of course, the dishonest steward isn't exactly building orphanages with the money.)

In other sermons, however, I have followed the second half of the parable, the moral of the story, as it were, which views this confusing tale as a *contrast* story. Shouldn't we avoid this type of reliance on money, deals, and questionable connections? Jesus says, "If then you have not been faithful in the dishonest wealth, who will entrust to you the true riches?" After all, the church is at its worst when imitating the ways of the secular world. We have our suspicions that some of these spectacularly successful preachers have taken some moral shortcuts. The minister is not an entrepreneur or an entertainer but a humble shepherd. Bottom line: "You cannot serve God and mammon."

Are these our only two choices: imitation or disapproval? There is a third way.

If you put your ear to this parable, you will catch the almost palpable sense of crisis surrounding it. There is no preamble to this story; it begins with a bang or, as the ancients said, *in medias res*, in the middle of things: "You're fired! Hand over your accounts," the master says, "and turn in your password." In another such parable the Lord says to a man who lives for worldly goods, "You fool, tonight I want your life!"

The story of the dishonest steward is about recognizing a crisis when you see one. In Greek, the word for "crisis" means judgment. It's the moment in which you decide what sort of person you are. You've got to serve somebody. Who will it be? At the crisis point in medicine, the patient will either recover or die. According to the reputedly Chinese proverb, a crisis is a "dangerous opportunity."

The kingdom of God comes in a crisis. By "kingdom" we mean Jesus. For in Jesus God is real and holds the claim check on each of our lives. His kingdom is a vast network of persons, communities, opportunities, and dangers in which God is suddenly and without warning—*here*.

Jesus is the Crisis of God. Suddenly, he is *here*, asking the big questions. In his earthly ministry, the best responses came from gentiles, widows, sinners, poor people—and a petty crook. *They all stand for us.*

They recognized a dangerous opportunity when they saw it. To those who thought they were religious, he said, "You never knew the time of your visitation." God came calling, and you didn't open the door.

This story is not a lesson in God-pleasing finance. Nor is it a warning against the dangers of handling money. It's something better and more redemptive. It's a strange little model of God's visitation in our lives. We are perplexed by the dishonest steward because we are perplexed about ourselves. But this mysterious parable—someone has called it "the hardest parable"—offers the clearest of messages. It tells us how to get saved.

The dishonest steward usually comes off second best to his parabolic cousin, the prodigal son, whose story is told in the preceding chapter. The prodigal "comes to himself," and thanks to Luke's wonderful powers of storytelling, we are made privy to his conversion and his decision to return to his father's house. We actually *hear* the prodigal's interior monologue. We are permitted to watch a mind as it changes in a way that is unique in the Gospels. But if you look at the *structure* of both parables, you make an amazing discovery: they are the same story!

In each story the leading character—the son or the steward—"squanders" the wealth of others. It is a rare word. Can it be accidental that Jesus uses the same word to describe the failures of both men? They both toss away something they already possess. The two stories share the same elements: the hero in both is not a very likable person. In both, the protagonist provokes a crisis by his greedy behavior. Both men quickly descend into chaos. Both reflect inwardly on their terrible situations. Both decide to do something about it. And both find their way home.

What am I saying? The two parables teach the same gospel: *God can save anybody.* God can save a callow kid who insults his father, and God can save a scam artist who knows a crisis when he sees one. God can save us too, wherever we fit on that spectrum. Like the prodigal, we can be welcomed home by the father. Like the steward, we can be "commended" by the master.

If we overlook a few unsavory points on the steward's record and grade him only on a pass-fail basis, he barely earns a pass. But in the kingdom of God, *barely* is more than enough to set off a huge celebration!

Jesus is the Crisis of God. How ironic that the church should use this parable as an excuse to compromise with the world and to play the world's game. Ironic because the one who tells the story represents the very antithesis of compromise. At every opportunity to save himself, he chose another route. He was approved by God not for his uncanny ability to work the system but for his utter faithfulness. Our lives now turn on him, as the whole world turns on the axis of his cross. Even now, he confronts us not with proven methods of success but with a loaf of bread and a cup of wine.

The evangelist Luke is clearly critical of the steward's behavior. Luke most likely received the parable and then added a few lines of interpretation at the end. Verses 9–13 are a little sermon with three separate points he has added to the story. They seem to reflect the evangelist's misunderstanding or criticism of the story as Jesus originally told it. He adds a warning from Matthew's version of the Sermon on the Mount: you cannot serve God and money. True enough, but this is a story about getting saved.

In the final verses, it is the evangelist himself who is playing the role of the elder brother in the parable of the prodigal son, who also looks down his nose at his brother's behavior and disapproves of his father's generosity. The elder brother, who apparently believes that since he's never been to the far country, he's never been lost.

He reminds me of *me*, or should I say *us*, whose theology of grace comes with an invisible filter that removes virtually everyone but people like us. But then, those who have played it safe often have a harder time comprehending God's grace than those who are in desperate need of it.

In our time, no one has seen this more clearly than the writer Flannery O'Connor. In her parabolic short story "Revelation," Mrs. Ruby Turpin finds herself in a doctor's small waiting room, where she takes harsh inventory of the people seated around her. The adjectives that flow through her head are "common," "ugly," "peculiar," "fat," and "mean," but most of all, "trash." Why should a good Christian woman like Ruby Turpin be clumped together with such trash? When one of the patients in the room, a disturbed young woman, assaults her and calls her a "warthog from hell," Mrs. Turpin is suddenly seized by her own crisis and forced to take stock of herself. Later, when she returns to her farm, she has a mystical vision in which she sees all the people in the waiting room and many others enrolled in a heavenward procession. She doesn't like what she sees because there is plenty of "trash" in that procession, rising on a lavender highway to heaven. She realizes that she is one of them herself, no better than the rest.

Whatever vices and virtues they might have had are being burned away. Ruby can hear the souls as they climb toward the stars singing hallelujah. God has found her too. She has become one of them.

As have we all.

24

You Must Forgive

*"If the same person sins against you seven times a day,
and turns back to you seven times and says, 'I repent,' you
must forgive."*

—LUKE 17:3–6

What do you think is the hardest thing about being a Christian?
Perhaps you have never put it that way, or, more likely, it's one of
those artificial questions that only preachers ask. But try to answer
it anyway.

When I was a boy, I thought the hardest thing was sitting in
church and listening to sermons. Boredom is as hard on children as
it is on adults. Later, as a religion major, I thought it was the super-
naturalism of Christianity, the idea that there is a heaven above, a hell
below, a child born of a virgin, a dead man come to life. Now, as an
older man, I confess it is something like the crucial significance of the
smallest things, of words and choices I once thought unimportant to
my heart and the hearts of others.

It is not heaven and hell or the enormity of the universe that we
are struggling with but something much closer, something to which
we have a more passionate resistance. The challenge of Christianity
is to live in such a way that contradicts our own deepest instincts.
Nowhere in the Gospels does Jesus say, "Follow your own moral instincts" or "Just do what comes naturally." Come to think of it, there
is no law of nature or inner voice reminding me to love someone

I don't like. It is no accident that the hardest thing comes to us not as an instinct but as a command: "You must forgive."

The disciples and Jesus are on a long journey toward Jerusalem, which we insiders know means the cross. They are walking and talking, and Jesus is telling stories. We are walking just behind them, as it were, listening in. Jesus has just told a great story about a rich man who gets scorched in hell and a poor beggar with sores all over his body who receives an eternal reward in the bosom of Abraham. That was a good one. Any more like that, Rabbi? "Sure," says Jesus. "Listen to this one. If someone close to you, like a brother or sister, a spouse or a roommate, does you dirt seven times in one day, you must—get this—you *must* forgive them seven times."

Got any other stories, Rabbi?

That's when the disciples say, "Increase our faith." Jesus seems to be saying, "Does forgiveness sound absurd to you? Then let me tell you about the absurdity of faith. If you had only a pinch of faith, you could take a mulberry tree and plant it in the ocean—that's how contrary to nature it is to live the forgiving life."

Forgiveness happens through a change of heart and an orderly exchange of words. It includes a wound, an apology, an absolution, and a gesture of restitution. Forgiveness is a transaction. It's a two-way, walkie-talkie word in which each party loses something: one admits wrong, the other gives up judgment. Both lose the right to hate. And in their mutual loss, something new is created. We need words to do this, but, since we know that we are going to lose something if we say the words, we try to do it without words. We would rather move nonverbally from dirty looks to benign silence to a friendly gesture and finally, but grudgingly, to a normalization of relations. No need to say anything.

But the Bible clings tenaciously to the word. The word is effective, performative. God's word doesn't merely describe things as they are, but it makes things happen. God said, "Let there be . . . and there was." Jeremiah says about the gods of a neighboring tribe (and this is the ultimate prophetic put-down), "Their gods are like scarecrows in a cucumber field, and they cannot speak." Somewhere in the wedding you really expect to hear the words, "I pronounce you husband and wife." And if you don't hear them, you're not sure anything has changed.

Most worship services are full of verbal transactions. We say, "The peace of the Lord be with you." And, miraculously, God's peace comes among us. In some services, the leader says, "In the name of Jesus Christ, you are forgiven," and the congregation responds, "In the name of Jesus Christ, you are forgiven." It's not only in the music or the sermon that something happens in the service, but in the act of mutual forgiveness a small transaction takes place and we are changed.

When the element of genuine change is missing, we have formalism—it's only words. It's the transactive element that seems to be missing from the recent spate of corporate and political apologies. Lately, one Protestant denomination apologized to African Americans for more than a century of institutional racism. I belong to a denomination that recently apologized to the Jews for remarks Martin Luther made. Not long ago the nation of Japan apologized for World War II, at about the same time the United States refused to apologize for dropping the atom bombs. A few years ago, the president of the United States apologized to African Americans for slavery, a move that drew both praise and criticism. Criticism, because without genuine change, any apology is hollow. Sometimes an apology is no apology, as when someone says, after sending out a racist or homophobic tweet, "I'm sorry if anyone was offended" (which means, if you are offended, it's your own fault).

Genuine forgiveness happens in a community of people who are walking with Jesus on the way to the cross. This is who we are: a community of forgiven and therefore forgiving people. We don't practice confession and absolution because we think it's therapeutic or because we agree with the hoary adage, confession is good for the soul.

In the interest of mental health, a man in New York City established a telephone "confession hotline." The idea is that anyone can call in, night or day, to make a confession. The anonymous confessions, so I'm told, are heart-wrenching not only in their pathos but also because they are not followed by absolution and reconciliation. One night a man called in to confess that when he was in Vietnam he had given his wedding ring as payment to a prostitute. From somewhere out there in the darkness of the city, he had to say that. Something must have been lifted from him. But with no assurance of absolution and no gracious welcome home, what remains but for the darkness to close in again?

In Greek, the word "forgive" means "to send away." It's hard for us to believe that some of the horrible things we've done or that have been done *to* us could be "sent away." Nothing disappears that easily, unless it's the perfect sentence or paragraph accidentally "sent away" into virtual space.

There are places in Scripture where God promises to remember always and never to forget, as when the Lord says to Israel, "Can a nursing mother forget her young? I will never forget you." And there are places in the same Scripture where the same God vows with equal vehemence to remember nothing: "I will forgive their iniquity and remember their sin no more."

What God forgets is our stupid sins. What God remembers is his love for us.

Not only is it hard to believe that sins could be forgiven, we question whether certain sins *ought to* be forgiven. Does the battered woman forgive the batterer seven times a day because he says, "Honey, I'm sorry"? Should the abused child forgive its abusers? There are many among us who have suffered such wrongs. They can only cry, "Never again!" For them, the command "You must forgive" adds a second burden to an already wounded emotional life. First, the injury, now the command to forgive it. Haven't we finally learned to just say NO to forgiveness?

If you receive an easy answer to such questions, you can be sure it's wrong. What can we say to the fellow pilgrim who has been abused? We uphold her in every way and assure her that an abuser's repentance, if it is genuine, cannot/must not be a tool of manipulation. Forgiveness is meant as a release, not an obligation to further break your spirit or to crush you when you practice it. Genuine forgiveness is the gift of God for the people of God. It is a little dying and rising transacted between those who are on the way. It is given to people who may be stunned and hurting, who aren't always able to decide which crimes are unforgivable, which wrongs can never be sent away, who to forgive, and who to hate. It's so incomprehensible a gift that it comes to us as a command.

The command to forgive is like the command not to kill or steal. Do we begin by creating a web of exceptions, by defining the circumstances when it is permissible or legal for us to kill or to steal? Or do we take these words from Jesus as guidance for a long journey, recognizing that they are greater than we are, and try to live by them? There's a sentence in one of C. S. Lewis's diaries: "Last week, while at prayer, I suddenly discovered . . . that I had really forgiven someone I had been trying to forgive for over 30 years."

Some years ago, radio commentator Terry Gross interviewed an elderly British officer named Lomax who, during World War II, was mercilessly beaten and tortured by his captor. Miraculously, forty-five years after the war Lomax tracked down his tormentor, fully intending, as he admits, to do him some harm. Finally, the two old men met, one the former interrogator, one the victim. To the astonishment and bewilderment of the victim, however, the perpetrator repented and asked for forgiveness. This was not in the fifty-year-old script! To further complicate matters, the two men got on well together and began to enjoy one another's companionship, all the while with this terrible issue hanging over them. One thing was clear to both men: a word was needed.

Finally, after three weeks, Lomax took pen in hand and wrote out a bill of forgiveness, went to the man, and read it to him. The interviewer asked him, "What did it feel like for you to forgive your enemy?" He replied, "It was good. A burden was lifted." Something in him was "sent away" as well.

We really aren't competent to design our own moral universe. If you want to see a model of forgiveness, you must look ahead in the story. The next mention of forgiveness in Luke's Gospel occurs on a Friday afternoon. It erupts from the parched lips of a dying man, "Father, forgive them." They don't even know enough to say "I'm sorry."

As I listened to Terry Gross's interview, I waited for her to ask the theological question. *Why* did you forgive? Where did you get the resources to forgive? She didn't ask it, but I know the answer. The answer is as absurd as planting a tree in the ocean, as absurd as a dead messiah raised by the power of God. These little transactions are like an endless card game we play with parents, spouses, children, siblings, roommates, even with ourselves. What are they but little versions of Jesus's death and resurrection? They are small but not insignificant reenactments of what happened to him once and for all time.

Something in us dies. Is it hate, fear? And something in us is born. Is it hope? freedom? The necessary word is spoken, and for a moment, at least, the screen turns a lovely blue. All that trash between us, in us, and behind us is sent into space. Gone.

"Lord, increase our faith."

25

THE HEART OF A HEARTLESS WORLD

*"So you also, when you have done all that you were ordered
to do, say, 'We are worthless slaves; we have only done what
we ought to have done!'"*

—LUKE 17:7–10

When Jesus came proclaiming the rule of God, he did so by telling stories in which it was hard to find God. His stories were a little like the children's book *Where's Waldo?* As some of you know, you must look very hard to find Waldo. He's everywhere, yet he's hidden in the most ridiculous places. When it comes to Jesus's stories, you have to search just as hard to see God—at least, to see God the way many of us were taught to see him. That is, as a supremely powerful (older) king who helps you feel reassured and protected.

Today's parable is not a feel-good story. Any story that begins "Who among you would say to your slave . . . ?" does not promise much comfort. "Who among you" is not the same as "Once upon a time." "Once upon a time" is a signal not to worry; "relax," it seems to say, "this will be about the past. It won't involve you." "Who among you," on the other hand, sets our sensory-motor apparatus aquiver. It fairly screams, "Avoid eye contact at all costs! This could be about you."

God does not appear as a character in the parables, any more than God is a visible, three-dimensional participant in our lives. Yet God is everywhere in the parables, just as God is everywhere in our lives. The message of the parables is simple: if you can't find God in the pots and pans of the real world—in the ordinary conflicts, celebrations, and concerns of daily life—you have missed out on something real and wonderful. That something Jesus calls the kingdom of God.

Jesus's parables are small models of the world as he found it. Instead of being made of wood and glue, his models are made of words. His stories are "secular"; that is, they depict the world as we experience it, and not as we wish it to be. His stories feature stupid, greedy people: judges who care nothing for justice, crooked money managers, insolent children, and the idle rich. They are also stories of people who have been beaten down and abused: poor widows, beggars, the unemployed—and slaves.

Given the reality of slavery in our nation's history and in our world today, the prominent role of slaves in Jesus's parables is troubling. We want to close our ears to it. We wouldn't mind returning to the older and inaccurate translation of the word for slave, "servant."

Jesus is addressing a well-to-do audience made up of people who will not be shocked by the phrase "your slave." They are like many of us first-world people who are comfortable with supervising the services of others. Many of us are also providers of service. Orders are given, and we must do what is expected of us. In our society, unlike ancient Palestine, one person may be a supervisor in one setting and a service provider in another. A flight attendant is expected to serve others in his or her professional capacity but on the next day be "served" by a hairstylist or a garage mechanic. It's complicated.

Jesus's parable is pitched toward those who give the orders. They are the ones who will feel the sting. The slave comes in after plowing all day and feeding the animals. Jesus asks, who among you will say, "Sit down, my good man, you must be tired. Let me serve you"? The expected answer from a slaveholding group of listeners is "Nobody!" Rather, he continues, you will order your employee to do his job. And when he obeys his master's command, why should he be thanked for doing what is expected of him?

In exactly four sentences, Jesus has constructed a model of a heartless world. It is the world of a hardscrabble Palestinian farmer and his one solitary slave who works the fields by day and runs the house by night. This is not *Downton Abbey* with liveried butlers and maids in ruffled uniforms, but something far uglier. These two stock characters are locked in a master-slave relationship that does not include friendship, kindness, or civility. The story offers no hint of gratitude or respect, no aura of spirituality, and no clue to the presence of God. It lacks heart.

The severity of the scene stands in sharp contrast to the modern habit of personalizing our own patron-server relationships with a veneer of cordiality. We pretend that we care about those who are paid to do our bidding. Sometimes we say they are "like family." And those who wait at table must pretend that they care about us as persons. We pretend that in a democratic society we are all on an equal footing. But when those who serve do their job, who will say to them, "Why don't you sit down and rest? Let us help you. We want to get to know you as a person." The parable gives the answer: nobody. Jesus has constructed a realistic model not only of his social world but also of ours.

It's a heartless little story Jesus tells, because we believe that everyone deserves to be thanked for their work and rewarded for it. If there are no rewards, why stay late at the office or in the shop? Why mortgage the house to send your child to the best school if there is no gratification down the line? When she joins the premier firm in the city, is it only a parental fantasy that she will turn to you and say, "Dad, Mom, you made this possible. Thank you"?

Every parable features an unexpected twist, a *gotcha* (*gotcha* is the language of the kingdom). In the first three sentences of this parable, the listeners—and that includes you and me—are cast in the role of the master. Who among us would bother to provide extra rewards to those who merely do their jobs?

In the last verse, however, the story makes a hard turn on its tiny axis, and we, the former masters, become the slaves. "So you also, when you have done all that you were ordered to do, say, 'We are worthless slaves; we have done only what we ought to have done!'" Once again, the word "slaves" jars us, because now it's being applied to us. With our national history of slavery, and knowing as we do that enslaved people helped build the nation, how can we stand to hear the phrase "worthless slaves" without rejecting it out of hand?

Jesus's strategy toward us has changed. In the second half of this story, he is no longer offering a model of Palestinian society but an equally challenging model of discipleship in a heartless world! Jesus makes a simple but severe comparison: just as an enslaved person must obey the master with no expectation of reward, the disciple obeys Jesus with no other expectation than a cross. With the incentive of reward gone, all that remains is the stark reality of obedience. The philosopher Nietzsche made fun of Christianity as a "religion of slaves." Nietzsche didn't know how right he was.

I know a woman. She works for a company called Home & Health, Inc. Because she is a professional, she makes a point to wear her blue scrubs every day as she makes her rounds all over the county. She enters the poorest homes and double-wides, teaching the infirm, disabled, and stroke victims how to get dressed, make their beds, and cook dinner. Sometimes she cleans up messes and serves breakfast, even though she is a professional. She is always on her own. There is no audience to admire her virtue; she hears no cosmic applause. She will not write a book about her ministry. Even her clients don't always express their gratitude. She does her good works in a silent and unresponsive universe.

She is not like many of us, especially the professionals among us, who are more than capable of good deeds so long as they are met with public approval. It's as if the work itself has a hold on her. In her own quiet way, she has broken through the performance/reward syndrome.

This year the university where I work gave each member of its freshman class two gifts. One was an iPod, which is a device for organizing your music and making it instantly available to you. The other gift was a book about Dr. Paul Farmer, the Pulitzer Prize–winning *Mountains beyond Mountains*. Farmer is a graduate of our university and a public health doctor who has devoted his professional life to serving the poor in Haiti.

No wonder the freshmen seem confused. Here is a university that promises its graduates incredible rewards if they do well, *and, at the very same time*, recommends a vocation with no tangible rewards. One voice promises, you can have it all when you want it. Another summons us to a life of service. Two roads crossing, then diverging.

Parable says, make up your mind!

After Paul Farmer had been serving in Haiti for a while, he began wearing a large wooden cross over his shirt. I think it was his way of saying, "The idea of serving others is not original with me." Once there was a man who made service his way of life. He came not to be served but to serve and to give his life a ransom for many. Who among you would want a life outside his life?

One of the most offensive phrases in this story is "what we ought to have done," which the RSV mercilessly condenses as "our duty." Duty alone is a stern taskmaster. Ask the servicemen and -women in Afghanistan about duty. Ask doctors and nurses who tend the sick at great risk to themselves. Ask the mom and dad who give themselves daily for their profoundly disabled child. They may not call it duty, but they would agree with Annie Dillard: "How we spend our days, of course, is how we spend our lives."

Paradoxically, the only way to do your duty is to discover something greater than duty. The child's parents know what that something is. And so do we. This parable would be unbearable if it taught nothing but duty. It would be unbearably severe were it not for the One who tells the story. The One who emptied himself and took the form of an enslaved person, who after supper girded himself with a towel and acted out a parable of love by washing his disciples' feet.

On that same night he said to his disciples, "I do not call you slaves any longer . . . but I have called you friends." Then he went to the cross and confirmed that friendship for all eternity. And with that, we find the heart in our heartless world.

26

Hunger and Hope

Taking the five loaves and the two fish, he looked up to heaven, and blessed and broke the loaves, and gave them to his disciples to set before the people.

—MARK 6:30–44

In my first parish, during the holy moments of silent prayer in the eleven o'clock service, I could have sworn I heard my parishioners' stomachs growling. At the time, I decided that sitting in church makes people hungry. But the truth is, we come to church because we are already hungry and hope to be fed. Together, hunger and hope make us human.

We are among the fortunate few who possess enough food to eat three times each day (and sometimes more), and therefore we tend to take the blessing of nourishment for granted. We say our prayers before each meal, of course, but often in a perfunctory manner. On other occasions, such as Thanksgiving or Christmas, we compose our prayers more carefully in order to take in the fullness of the blessings. In harder times, when we are housebound or grieving and friends bring their casseroles and loaves of bread to our table, we are reminded of the close connection between food and friendship, hunger and hope. Then we say with the psalmist, "O taste and see how gracious the Lord is."

Most of the world's people do not eat three times a day or even twice a day. They are victimized by famine, poverty, war, and corruption. And as grains are increasingly used for biofuel and feed for cattle, the price of bread skyrockets worldwide. We have seen ordinary people in Bangladesh, Cameroon, Yemen, Mexico, Egypt, and the Philippines rioting, not for democratic elections but for affordable bread.

Closer to home, it's not unthinkable to come out of Harris Teeter or Whole Foods on a warm summer evening and to come face-to-face with a woman on the parking lot who says, "I've got three kids at home and no food. Will you help me?" You make a mental note that you have never met someone begging for food so close to the market before. It's as if the river's flood stage has reached a new high and should be recorded with a marker of some kind. In the Great Recession I heard a woman say, "The month is always longer than the money." What some of us once took for granted—three square meals—has become a matter of careful calculation.

The woman on the parking lot would have agreed with the disciples, "Lord, this is a lonely place."

The feeding of the five thousand is the only miracle of Jesus that is reported in all four Gospels (and Mark tells it twice!). *We* call it a miracle, although the text does not call it that. It's not as if Jesus said, "Now let me take you out to a lonely place so I can show you something spectacular." In fact, we don't know why he wanted to be alone, but we can guess. His friends may have just informed him about the beheading of John the Baptist, which is reported in the previous verses. My best guess is that he was stunned by grief and needed to get away. For, without a moment's hesitation, Jesus reacts like a person in acute distress. Let's go, he says. Where? Away from here. Anywhere. But as it often happens, when Jesus arrives at his place of retreat, the hunger is there waiting for him.

Why is this story told five times? Why did the early Christians draw crude pictures of the feeding of the five thousand on the walls of the catacombs beneath Rome? Is it because it's such an extraordinary miracle? No, there are more dramatic miracles. The reason is more basic. It's because we are always hungry, and God is always feeding us.

Fifteen summers ago, when our son was struggling with cancer, friends and coworkers brought food to our table in waves of compulsive generosity. Moroccan chicken, flank steak smothered in onions, veggie casseroles, peach cobbler made with delectable South Carolina peaches, Russian cream cake—even people we hardly knew brought us their signature dishes. All were gifts—the food and those who brought it. One person brought a jar of peanut butter and a knife. That summer we arrived at the most basic level of dependency, that of receiving nourishment from the hands of others. When done in community, this simple transaction signifies our relationship to God.

We don't simply eat for nourishment. In a very basic way, eating together cements relationships and friendships. The best days during our longest summer were the days when those delivering food stayed and joined us at table. Many a country church still has a picnic on the grounds replete with home-fried chicken, German potato salad, macaroni and cheese, summer squash, deviled eggs with paprika, nineteen kinds of Jell-O, and pecan pie. But it wouldn't be all that enjoyable if we didn't arrange our tables in squares so we could look at one another and tell old stories while we eat.

What could be better than eating with friends? But in the psalm for today, the psalmist takes our love of community a step further: "Thou preparest a table before me in the presence of mine enemies." Why would you need a *table* in the presence of your enemies? Why not a better lawyer than your enemy has, or a stronger army or a bigger gun? It means that when enemies (or strangers) meet, it is God who overcomes our natural inclination toward exclusion and sets before us a simple table.

When I was a teenager, I worked a summer construction job, the only Caucasian on a crew of ten. I wish I could report that we all ate our lunch together and had a kingdom of God experience, but I think it was as unimaginable to the nine as it was to me, the tenth, that we should share this human intimacy. I never said, "Mind if I join you?" They never said, "Why don't you join us."

Years later as a college student, I found myself stranded in the middle of the night in a Chicago train station. I had missed my train, and I was stuck. An African American family kindly offered me a ride, which I accepted. As we drove north on Interstate 94 toward Milwaukee, I said innocently, "I'm hungry, why don't we stop for breakfast." Their silence seemed to say, "Young man, you have no idea." We pulled into a still-segregated restaurant just off the highway. My new friends gave me their orders, I took them in, brought out the food, and we ate our breakfast in the car.

That episode must be long forgotten by them, but not by me. I thank God for that meal, for the instruction it provided, and the hope for a new future it inspired in me.

I believe that some meals can never be fully consummated on this earth. Even a breakfast of congealed eggs and cooling bacon devoured in a parked car has the potential to be something more than it is. It can be a revelation. An Almost Eucharist. This is true of Jesus's feeding of the five thousand. Its meager materials point us forward to another table and toward another feast. He took the five loaves and two dried fish, blessed them, broke them, and gave them to the disciples. Taking, blessing, breaking, giving—with these same verbs Mark later describes the Passover Jesus celebrated with his disciples. We repeat the very same verbs over the meal we are about to share.

A nineteenth-century materialist [Ludwig Feuerbach] coined the phrase, "You are what you eat." Christians are instinctively aghast at this claim because we know that we are creatures of God with God's spirit within us. We are much, much more than the proteins, fats, fruits, and grains we devour and process. But think about the phrase as you return from the communion table. Fed by the Lord, we are indeed what we eat. For he fills us not only with food but with himself.

We have a separate sacrament called Eucharist (and just how *separate* the church made it is another story), but *all* our eating and drinking is done in the presence of and by the mercy of a gracious God. In the earliest Christian community, the Eucharist occurred as a part of a communal meal. Consecrated bread and wine, yes, but also the first century's version of chicken, greens, cornbread, and all the fixin's.

Whether you're eating a picnic with friends, giving thanks over a plastic tray in a hospital room, or coming to this altar, there is only one table and one great feast. God is the host. Whether at the grandest of meals or over comfort food at the local diner, we pray the same words from our liturgy, "Grace our table with your presence and give us a foretaste of the feast to come."

Once we do this, our attitude toward eating and drinking will never be the same. *How* we eat and *how much* we eat, *with whom* we eat, and our resolve to feed *others*—all—become sacred questions and holy acts. For all this eating and drinking occurs from the hand of God.

We don't understand why Jesus fed the people as he did. Why not simply cause the bread to drop from heaven like pixie dust? Why not a daily ration of manna? Why not follow the devil's advice and turn the stones in the desert into bread? Instead, he tells the disciples (who always stand for *us*) to feed the people. To which the disciples respond with their usual insight: "What do you expect us to do, go out and buy enough food for this great Woodstock of hungry strangers?" What do you expect us to do? To which Jesus calmly replies, "I expect you to feed them."

With these words he is establishing the church as a distribution center of God's blessings. It's been done before: The pagan emperor Julian the Apostate was forced to admit, "The godless Galileans feed not only their poor but ours also." Fifteen hundred years ago, the great archbishop of Constantinople, John Chrysostom, bragged that his church was feeding three thousand people a day! By enlisting us as partners in this act of mercy, Jesus is certifying that this is much more than a one-off miracle. It is our way of life.

About twenty years ago, a woman named Sara Miles walked off the sidewalk in San Francisco into an Episcopal church and took a seat in the congregation. She was unbaptized and not a churchgoer. At the words "Jesus invites everyone to his table," she got up with the rest and received the bread and wine of the Eucharist. She did it on an impulse. Like many of us, she had come to church with a deep and unacknowledged hunger. That impulsive decision eventually led her to conversion, baptism, and a ministry of feeding hungry people. She organized a food pantry that eventually involved scores of volunteers and provided meals for thousands of families throughout the Bay Area. Sara Miles forges a link between the church's Eucharist and the church's mission. It is a way of saying, it's all one Hunger and all one Food and all one Hope.

She imagines the church as a transformer site where all the hungers of humanity meet the lines of hope that run from God. In her memoir, *Take This Bread*, she sums it up this way: "I was, as the prophet said, hungering and thirsting for righteousness. I found it as the eternal and material core of Christianity: Body, blood, bread, wine, poured out freely, shared by all. I discovered a religion rooted in the most ordinary yet subversive practice: a dinner table where everyone is welcome, where the despised and outcasts are honored."

It is food for thought among us, the proprietors of a new parish hall; a state-of-the art, stainless-steel kitchen; and a renovated sanctuary. How are these facilities connected to one another? Is there an invisible conduit from our altar to our kitchen? And from our kitchen, to whom? How can we become a more effective distribution center, not merely for food but for care and ministry to our neighbors, many of whom find themselves in a lonely place, like sheep without a shepherd?

We live a mere thirty miles from the capital of our state, where it is against the law to feed a homeless person in a public park. What are the well-fed to do? The Lord says, *you feed them*. Not only here from this eucharistic table but in other places of hunger, need, and hopelessness: *You feed them*. Not only in the company of friends but in the presence of enemies, strangers, and people you don't understand.

You feed them. And I will feed you.

27

THE BIG PICTURE

From now on, therefore, we regard no one from a human point of view. . . . So if anyone is in Christ, there is a new creation: everything old has passed away; see, everything has become new!

—2 CORINTHIANS 5:16–21

Thirty years ago, a space probe known as Voyager I was making its way past the planet Pluto on its way out of our solar system. An astronomer and astrophysicist named Carl Sagan persuaded NASA to rotate the craft so that it could look over its shoulder, as it were, the way you might do when leaving home for the last time. He wanted one last picture of "home" from four billion miles away. It is a famous photo. In it the earth appears as a microscopic smudge in a darkened sky. Much smaller than a grain of salt. One-tenth of one pixel among 700,000 pixels. Sagan called it the "Pale Blue Dot."

In his poetic commentary on the photo, he wrote, "Look again at that dot. That's here. That's home. That's us. . . . Every saint and sinner in the history of our species lived there—on a mote of dust suspended in a sunbeam. Our imagined self-importance, the delusion that we have some privileged position in the Universe, is challenged by this point of pale light. Our planet is a lonely speck in the great enveloping cosmic dark. In all this vastness, there is no hint that help will come from elsewhere to save us from ourselves."

The Pale Blue Dot is a place to start as we try to make sense of the peculiar statement Paul makes in our text. He says he no longer views things from a human point of view. Like the scientist Sagan, he sees how big the creation is and how little we are and how foolish we appear when we claim to be lords of the Pale Blue Dot.

Paul's new perspective doubtless goes back to something that happened to him years before. You may remember that he was on his way to arrest some Christians in Damascus when he was blinded by a bright light and heard a voice from above. As far as we know, Paul never saw or met Jesus in the flesh, which means the voice from heaven was an introduction of sorts: "Saul, Saul, I am Jesus. You know, the one you are persecuting." It was enough to change Saul to Paul and to open his eyes in amazement.

Writing some years later, he is like a person who has had both cataracts removed. What was shrouded in a fine mist suddenly sparkles with newfound clarity. This is what Paul sees: "In Christ God was reconciling the world to himself."

The Greek language has a perfectly good word for "world," planet Earth. But Paul uses another word instead, one that is familiar to us, due in part to its popularization by Carl Sagan: *kosmos*. Cosmos is nothing less than everything: stars, planets, time, history, culture, geography—you and me. Moreover, this thing Paul refers to as cosmos belongs together with something even bigger than cosmos. That bigger something he calls God. You put God and cosmos together in the same picture, you have something beautiful.

You have the Big Picture.

Just before church this morning, when no one was looking, I put a tiny piece of tumbled blue glass on the altar. I wanted to symbolize for myself and those of you in the fifty-second row how little—and precious—our home really is. I put it on the altar because it belongs to a great and magnificent God. I wanted to help you see the Big Picture.

Of course, there are times when the last thing we want to consider is the Big Picture. When you're in a meeting or a discussion group and the conversation grows heated, there's always someone who says, "Let's stop for a moment and look at the Big Picture." Then, the Big Picture serves as a diversion from problems for which we have no solution. You want to say, "I have an idea; why don't we solve a problem first, *any* problem, and save the Big Picture for the coffee break?"

Fervently, we wish to solve the problems of racism in our community, distrust among Jews, Christians, and Muslims, or the problem of privilege on an elite campus. But the questions overwhelm us.

If Paul were to join the meeting, I believe he would say something like this: "These are good questions, and they must be answered. But I'm wondering why you always begin at the wrong end of every issue. Have you ever thought of starting with the answer instead of the question?"

What if we followed Paul's lead and started with the *answer* and allowed it to shape the question? We hardly ever ask the right questions. We rarely ask questions the answer to which is "obedience," "Trinity," "reconciliation." What if we began our consideration of life in community from our Christian convictions? What if we began with the embrace rather than exclusion?

Then, our thesis sentence is not "I don't trust you" but "We are baptized." Not "You are different" but "We are made in the image of God"? Not "You are too old" but "new creation!"? What might happen if we started from the answers?

The Paul we meet in 2 Corinthians is dealing with a congregation plagued by every conceivable division—doctrinal, liturgical, interpersonal, socioeconomic, and, just for good measure, a case of incest. Otherwise a perfect church. There are those in his congregation who dispute the very thesis sentence of everything Paul stands for, namely, the saving cross of Christ. Worst of all—and this is every preacher's nightmare—a whispering campaign is under way to the effect that our man Paul is an effective letter writer but not much of a preacher. "For they say, 'His letters are weighty and strong, but his bodily presence is weak, and his speech contemptible.'"

In the face of conflicts that would unhinge any normal human being, Paul has this uncanny ability to see the Big Picture. To the fragmented Corinthians he writes, "If anyone is in Christ [and aren't we all?] there is a new creation." The Greek text is even more explosive. It reads, "If anyone is in Christ—new creation!" In Galatia, where the divisions are just as deep, he once again begins with the answer: "There is neither Jew nor Greek, slave nor free, male nor female, but you are all one in Christ Jesus." Then, on to Colossae, where the congregation is torn between new age religions and the cross of Christ. To them he writes, "He himself is before all things, and in him all things hold together."

There was another Big Picture man, Martin Luther King, who was fond of saying, "The arc of the moral universe is long, but it bends toward justice." That's a high-altitude pronouncement if ever there was one, but I believe it was Dr. King's way of aligning his many tribulations on behalf of justice with something larger than himself and his organization. He could make a sweeping generalization about the moral bent of the universe not because he was an astronomer but because he was a theologian. Paul might have put it this way: the arc of God's cosmos is long. See how it bends toward reconciliation.

But what does that mean on the ground? Must the devil be in the details? It means that when you work for justice and stand up for those who are being shot down, you are flowing with the designs of God and not against them. It means that when you are outraged by sins committed against the cosmos—by the eighty-eight pounds of plastic found in the belly of a beached whale (as reported last week in the *New York Times*), by the obscenity of starvation on a green planet, by the senseless shootings across the country—your anger follows the divine curve. You are moving with the grain of the spiritual universe and not against it.

There is a Big Picture in human relationships too. And here it gets very complicated. Reconciliation is a three-step process. First comes repentance, then forgiveness, and finally reconciliation. The process includes language, which for many is the hardest part. It includes actual words, the equivalents of "I'm sorry," "I forgive you," and "I love you," usually in that order. Of course, some people can toss off the right words with little trouble, but for others it's like pulling teeth.

As a case study, consider the prodigal son in today's Gospel lesson. The prodigal is down on his luck. He is convinced that he needs a good speech in order to win over the old man. We find him in the pigsty, rehearsing: "Father, I have sinned against you and heaven, and I am no longer worthy to be called your son." He intuitively understands that he must say *something*. But to the father, it seems more important that the boy has *turned* toward home. For when he arrives, his father is waiting for him with a bear hug before he can get a word out. The prodigal is never reinstated as "son" because he was never out of the orbit of the father's love. And neither are we.

We have just heard the best commentary on this story sung by our guests in the Swati language. These are the words of "Ngena Nawe" in English:

> Here is the door
> The door to life
> It has been opened for you
> It's wide open for you
> Enter, you are welcome . . .

The third Sunday in Lent is traditionally known as Refreshment Sunday, probably for the joyous relief offered by the happy ending of the parable of the prodigal son. A boy and his father are reconciled. The end. But there is another son. And he can neither forgive nor reconcile with his brother. And because he can't reconcile with his brother, he is compelled to turn his back on his father and the music, dancing, and feasting in the father's house. *His* house. His *home*. The Gospel for Refreshment Sunday ends on a decidedly unrefreshing note.

The new creation in personal relationships has a beauty all its own. I once caught a glimpse of it in a mediation between a teenaged son and his father. It was a long time ago, decades. Admittedly, the event is fuzzy to me, but what I felt when I witnessed it is not. As I remember it, the boy was rebellious. The father was a marine. Not a hopeful set of circumstances for reconciliation. The mediator said—unwisely, I thought—"Why don't each of you pull up your chairs and tell what you want from the other. What do you each want?" The boy began, and he had a considerable list: a decent car, a better sound system (a stereo as it was then known), no restrictions, no hassles. You can imagine.

Then it was the father's turn. I braced myself for what was sure to come. A haircut, new friends, lose the earring. But instead, the room got very quiet, and the marine said, "I want him to be my son." He didn't say it possessively but wistfully. That he could say it at all was only because the boy had never ceased to be his son. At that moment it felt as if something new had been created, and some new possibility for the future had made an appearance.

But sometimes reconciliation is impossible. The wounds are too deep. Life has moved on. Circumstances have changed. Perhaps one of the parties has died. Anyone can take the first step. You can distance-forgive. You can forgive the dead. You can forgive someone who doesn't want to be forgiven. You can love someone who doesn't love you back. You can open your arms even when there is no one there to be enfolded in them. It is the worst kind of emptiness. For we feel that we have fallen short of the final step, which is reconciliation.

Just then, Jesus stands in for the missing one, or puts himself in the path of hurtful actions whose consequences cannot be called back. He says, "You can't reconcile with that person or with that community because they are dead to you, but I am alive. I stand in for them. Reconcile with me." This is where the season of Lent is leading us: not only to deny ourselves but to open ourselves to others.

The goal is reconciliation. We are being carried toward something that has already been achieved on a cosmic scale. It happens in Christ. The poet John Donne understood our place in the cosmos when he wrote, "I am a little world made cunningly / of elements and an angelic sprite." In Christ, God descended through the stars to be made one of us. Like us, Jesus was also made cunningly, and of the same elements as we: oxygen, nitrogen, calcium, and love. He was made of the same capacities as we: the capacity for sadness, pain, anger, and joy, all cunningly assembled in one redemptive person.

Now when God looks at us, what does he see? What is the God's-eye view of little us? Is it the Pale Blue Dot, a gorgeous but insignificant speck on the palette of creation? Or, looking through the eyes of Christ, does the Creator see both the needs and the beautiful capacities in each one of us? In Jesus, the cosmic distance has been abridged. He is our home. Come home.

In him, the whole cosmos is singing,

> Here is the door.
> It is wide open for you.
> Do not be afraid.
> Come in, you are welcome.

28

"I Am Baptized"

In those days Jesus came from Nazareth of Galilee and was baptized by John in the Jordan. And just as he was coming up out of the water, he saw the heavens torn apart and the Spirit descending like a dove on him.

—MARK 1:9–11

When my mother was twelve years old, she got herself baptized. Her mother had been dead for about a year, and her father was a Kentucky railroad man who was gone most nights. She was essentially raising herself, if a child can do such a thing. One hot summer evening when she was home alone as usual, she went down to the neighborhood Baptist church where they were holding a revival. At first, she just sat in the back pew and watched. Up front there was a large pool of the coolest and most inviting water you could imagine, and right there in that sweltering church, people were splashing and diving beneath its surface. When the preacher in his waders cried out, "O sinners, come to the river of life," that was all she could stand, and the twelve-year-old girl bolted toward the water and was baptized. That night her sins were washed away, she joined Jesus and his church, and she was never alone again.

Her baptism was part ecstasy, part curiosity. Born of loneliness and performed among strangers, it did not follow the usual scenario for the sacrament as we know it. But then neither does the baptism of Jesus reported by Mark in his first chapter. For what he describes has ripples throughout the cosmos. When Jesus comes up out of the water, he sees the heavens open—the Greek verb says they were "ripped apart." (Likewise, at Jesus's death the veil of the temple will be "ripped apart.") The fabric of the everyday has been torn. Something has been breached. It's a revelation. A voice says to him, "You are my beloved son in whom I am well pleased."

In most traditions baptism is a grand but far from cosmic occasion. Relatives gather in the church. Pews are reserved. Grandmother's yellowed baptismal dress with its garniture of embroidered lace makes an appearance, its tiny buttons made of river pearl. With phones on *camera*, we celebrate the moments of our lives. Over it all the minister presides with benign expertise. Afterward, the food is wonderful.

We wouldn't have it any other way, but baptism gets reduced to something smaller and less potent than its portrayal in the New Testament. To some it's a ceremony of initiation, the first baby step on the long road to maturity. For Paul, however, it's something more dramatic. It is a drowning. The ritual asks us to imagine that this child, asleep on its mother's shoulder, is being buried with Jesus in death in order to be raised with him to newness of life. The child begins life's journey with a funeral—its own! As it turns out, baptism is not a step toward a contented life but a leap into the river with Jesus.

The poet Philip Larkin must have been thinking of the potency of water—to cleanse, kill, and give life—when he wrote,

> If I were called in
> To construct a religion
> I should make use of water.

In his discussion of baptism in the *Small Catechism*, Luther asks, "How can water do such great things?" then quickly answers, "It is not water alone." The question already betrays the modern tendency to break a mystery down into manageable parts capable of analysis. Many of us know too well the questions about baptism: How old must one be to be baptized? How much sin can a child have? How much faith can a baby have? How does the baby's faith relate to the faith of the witnesses? Luther's answer is a reminder that faith can't be quantified. He reminds us that the formula for baptism is not water plus personal faith, but water plus the word of God.

One afternoon a strange-looking preacher dressed up like Elijah the prophet appeared on the shores of the Jordan and said, "O sinners, come to the river," and another young man, his cousin, walked into the water and was baptized. We celebrate the baptism of Jesus in the Epiphany season because an epiphany is a revelation. The ordinary has been ripped open like a neatly wrapped Christmas present, and something extraordinary makes a brief appearance. Suddenly, we see something new about Jesus: he is the beloved Son of God.

We Christians understand our baptism in the mirror of Jesus's baptism. We are *in* him, we say, and he is *in* us. We have never been content to know a few facts about Jesus or to entertain selected truths about God. No, we are in him, as Paul says, we've put him on as a soldier girds himself for battle, or as we slip into a sweater on a chilly day.

Not many of us were baptized in a river, but if you have received Christian baptism, you have in fact been to the river with him. You too have slipped beneath the water. You've put the river on and let it cover you from head to foot. Baptism is our own soaking in the Jordan, when the voice from heaven says to us, "You are my daughter; you are my son. Welcome to my family. You will never be alone again."

As you might expect, baptism with Jesus does not come without a cost. If this sacrament is only a ceremony, it exerts no claim on our lives. Before the Civil War, many slaveholding Protestants effectively reduced the value of baptism to their slaves and its cost to themselves. They allowed their enslaved people to be baptized, but only with the explicit proviso that baptism would not entail political or social freedom. In other words, it would have no effect on the condition of one's actual life.

But baptism is larger and stronger than that. Listen in on any one of several baptismal liturgies, and you have a clue to the size of its claims. Many of them begin with what is known as the Renunciations:

> "Do you renounce Satan and all the spiritual forces of wickedness that rebel against God?"
> *"I renounce them."*
> "Do you renounce the evil powers of this world which corrupt and destroy the creatures of God?"
> *"I renounce them."*
> "Do you renounce all sinful desires that draw you from the love of God?"
> *"I renounce them."*

The minister seems to be asking, do you have any idea of what you are in for? Do you understand that with this act you are not joining the world but breaking with it? Do you realize there is such a thing as evil and that you have just enlisted in the fight against it? The Christian life begins with a declaration of war.

In one of Flannery O'Connor's stories, "A Temple of the Holy Ghost," a little Catholic girl—"the child"—lives with her parents and relatives in a small southern town amidst a sea of Protestants. She enjoys visiting the convent where one of the sisters always embraces her as she leaves. But every time she gets a hug, the crucifix on sister's belt gets mashed into the child's face. The reader is left to imagine how the gesture of love always leaves a mark. Baptism is like that. In Christ, God gives us a hug, but that act leaves the sign of the cross upon us to remind us of the one whose name we bear.

Many of us received a name when we were baptized. Not a number, a password, or a code, not a name to be misspelled, merged, and buried with all the other names. But in baptism we take the name Christian, to be worn on our sleeve and held in our heart.

The identity based on that relationship is a matter of faith. It remains even when you can't remember your baptism or reproduce the fervor that accompanied it. It's hard to imagine a more radical or absolute form of reliance on a Being outside your own jurisdiction. When Luther found himself in a crisis or depression, unable to sense his own salvation, he would stubbornly cling to an act performed outside his own agency or memory. Then he would roar, "I am baptized."

The question of identity is also a matter of context. In your familiar surroundings, you're pretty sure you know who you are. But go away to college, enlist in the military, move to a new neighborhood, or take a different job, and your identity seems to be up for grabs. You even look different to yourself. Of course, expensive colleges or big corporations will not be shy about telling you who you are. At the new-student orientation session, some dean or admissions officer will gush, "We have chosen you because you are the brightest and the best, the crème de la crème." What is left unspoken but understood is, "and you belong to us." On the other hand, if you're poor, of the wrong race, or otherwise marginalized, you may hear a different message: You are nobody.

To both messages we say *NO*: I renounce them. I am not the crème, and I am not a nobody. I am baptized!

The church, too, will not be shy about telling you who you are. You are brothers and sisters of the Lord Jesus. As he himself once said, "Whoever does my will is brother and sister and mother to me." But not only that—and this is the hard part—you are also brothers and sisters to one another. You haven't chosen your fellow Christians as your family any more than you chose your natural family, but your baptism has made it so. We have all been washed in the same tub. Christians are bonded to one another by water and the word.

We enter the river as lonely swimmers, as alone as the homebound or homesick (it's always dangerous to swim alone). We come out of the water with this difference: We know who we are. We are Christ's forgiven people. We are saved.We are baptized.

The "I" has become "We." We are family.

For All the Saints

29

GOD'S FACULTY

And I saw the holy city, the new Jerusalem, coming down out of heaven from God.

—REVELATION 21:1–4

Outside the little town of Chartres in France, you drive on ordinary country roads past ordinary farmhouses until you see something so extraordinary that your eyes disbelieve. For there, shimmering in the morning mist, is a church so supernaturally beautiful that it appears to be descending from heaven. At the first sight of it, you catch your breath and say something silly like, "Now that's what I call a church," but of course, what you mean is, "That's *the* church!" That's the church as it is portrayed in the book of Revelation, "coming down out of heaven, prepared as a bride." Triumphant, beautiful, transcendent.

Some years ago, I returned to a church I once served in the rural Midwest. It too is located on an ordinary oil-and-dirt road, in an ordinary cornfield, in sight of some ordinary farmhouses. However, my church does *not* appear to be descending from heaven, but its worn red bricks seem to grow up out of the soil. There are no tour buses in its parking lot, and it definitely does *not* shimmer in the morning mist. It is capped off not by a majestic tower but by a peeling steeple with a cross from which one arm is sadly missing.

These two churches are a parable of All Saints' Day. But they aren't really two churches but two dimensions of one church—the church above that lives by sight, and the church below that struggles by faith. In the church above, there is no suffering, mourning, or grief. No disease, no addiction, no violence, no heart monitors or infusion bags. In the church below—well, we're acquainted with its sins, its weaknesses, its vulnerability to persecution, and its tendency to persecute. In John Calvin's words, a *lacerated body*. Each church has its logo: the gilded throne surrounded by white-robed saints, and the one-armed cross of my old parish. They almost never meet except on All Saints' Day, the day the church sets aside to treasure the suffering and to imagine the glory.

There are two ways of getting to know the saints, just as there are two ways, let's say, of learning about impressionistic painting. You can take a course on impressionism and listen to lectures for a semester, or you can walk into a great art museum and stand agog in front of a forty-two-foot-wide Monet and let *it* explain what impressionism is all about. Some of us are grateful for the saints because we've read the book of Revelation or have studied church history. Others are grateful for the saints because we've lived in the presence of one person in whom the goodness of God was condensed and in whom the glory was visible, and that was enough. Our entire education in sainthood may have to come to us through the prism of one "for instance."

It might have been the grandmother who prayed you through a difficult childhood; the spouse or partner who believed in you when you didn't believe in yourself; the college chaplain who brought you to Christ just when you were sure you had outgrown God; the parents who sacrificed everything in order to give you opportunities they never had. God breathed on these embers, and they turned to radiance, just for you.

The funny thing is—none of them *knew* they were saints. They never applied for the job and would have been embarrassed by the title. Some of them are like the whiskey priest in Graham Greene's novel *The Power and the Glory*. He's a priest who keeps a mistress, drinks too much, and is often afraid, but despite government persecution he continues to hear confession and bring the Eucharist to poor villagers. Just before his execution, the whiskey priest worries that he is going to God empty-handed. The poor man doesn't even know he's a saint.

Among most Protestants sainthood never really caught on. We worried that the veneration of the saints might detract from salvation through Christ alone. We were confident that our personal faith was more than sufficient to get us through. But I suspect the real reason had more to do with radical arrogance than radical faith. The fact is, we didn't want to be shaped or formed in anyone's mold but our own. The work of believing is so important that we can only do it for ourselves. Mentors are for people who *need* mentoring. Big Brother and Big Sister programs are for kids at risk—not our kids. Higher education pays homage to the wisdom of others, of course, but its real mission is to teach students to think for themselves.

It is our custom to celebrate self-made men and women, captains of industry and arbiters of public opinion. That impulse continues in our admiration for those who have reinvented themselves. I remember a presidential debate some years ago in which one candidate asserted that his opponent had reinvented himself. It was not received as a compliment. Today, it's considered a mark of genius. Yesterday you were an insurance executive; today you're a holistic healer. Yesterday you were a disgraced politician; today you're Dancing with the Stars. You will be successful in proportion to the chutzpah with which you thumb your nose at your former identity.

When you stop and think about it, that's what many of the saints did too—they made 180-degree detours from one life into another. But instead of reinventing *themselves*, they were reinvented by God. In the fourth century, Martin of Tours was a soldier in the Roman army. One day he saw a beggar at the city gate of Amiens and he impulsively cut in two his *cappa*, his cloak, and covered the man with half of it. He proceeded to devote the rest of his life to being a *capalein*, a chaplain, to those in need.

In the late nineteenth century, Thérèse of Lisieux was a French teenager who became convinced that God's love is best practiced in "the little way" of everyday acts of kindness and mercy toward others. She once said, "Sufferings gladly borne for others convert more people than sermons"! By the time she gets around to writing her autobiography at the ripe old age of twenty-three, she has already dived so deeply into the ocean of God that she hardly mentions that she's dying of tuberculosis.

In the 1970s, a student named Paul Farmer attended this university, where he undoubtedly loitered in the quad, partied with friends, and worshiped in the basketball stadium. After medical school he founded an organization that brings free health care to the people of Haiti and other impoverished nations. Several years ago, on All Saints' Day, a priest in Boston—and one of Farmer's old fraternity brothers—said, "I know it embarrasses him when I say it, but Paul's a saint. . . . He models for us how to be a Christian, how to be human in these inhumane times."

The saints are our teachers. They are God's faculty. And here's what they teach: they teach the hardest subjects, the kind that, when you're honest with yourself you say, "I could use a tutor." They specialize in subjects that even the most powerful and best educated among us have not mastered and probably never will. They teach us how to forgive. They teach us how to say no to power. They teach us always to tell the truth. They teach us how to forget ourselves and serve others. But most of all, the saints teach us how to die.

As you know, the church doesn't observe the birthdays of the saints and martyrs but their death days. The story of any saint always begins with a terrible death and works its way backward. It's as if the community is asking, what exactly *is* it about this life that made this death so necessary, and so precious in the Lord's sight?

We are eager to learn from them and to tell others. In the second century, when a man named Polycarp of Smyrna was burned at the stake for his faith, the elders of his church were there taking notes. It's from them that we learn that he could have skipped his own funeral by saying two little words, "*Kurios Caesar*," Lord Caesar. The church has lived off his Great Refusal for two millennia. When the martyr Dietrich Bonhoeffer was finally summoned from his cell to be hanged, someone was there to watch him pray and to record his words: "For me this is the end but also the beginning of life." It was his last lecture. There were witnesses to Bishop Óscar Romero's murder in El Salvador. They can answer our question, what was it about his sacrifice that makes him a blessing to us?

I would include in our list of teachers those who are not otherwise commemorated. They are the ones who quietly incorporate the routines and the indignities of dying into their walk with Jesus and thereby transform that walk into a witness. They are people worth remembering. What would we do without them? How could we live in a world with victims only and no witnesses?

Some years ago, there was a movie featuring a little boy whose signature line was "I see dead people." The line freaked everybody out. For death is the ultimate taboo, the unmentionable subject in polite conversation. Better not to talk about it because you might say the wrong thing. Those who grieve are often stunned by the silence that surrounds their loss. For death is a private matter between you and your hospice nurse. Grief is a private matter between you and your therapist. Even hope is a private matter between you and your priest. Despair is a private matter between you and your own broken heart.

I had an old friend who used to say to me, "One thing is certain. We all die alone." (He said this just before he died with those who loved him gathered round his bed.) One listens politely to this "soft fatalism" among Christians while casting about for a more satisfying answer. Why should anyone, even a curmudgeonly Presbyterian, think that the drama of life and death is a solo performance? Look up! See the City of God with both its beauty and its human imperfections descending from the heavens. Look around! See the brothers and sisters. They are not spirits. Pray with them, weep with them, sing with them. Let them hold your hand. We don't have to be lonely in the family of God. And we do not die alone.

In the Roman world, the dead were buried outside the walls of the city in a necropolis of their own. It's the oldest form of segregation. Not "separate but equal" but "dead, therefore separate." But then, as Peter Brown tells it in *The Cult of the Saints*, the church did something unthinkable in a pagan society. It said, *we see dead people*, and, behold, they are good. Christians began taking their bread and wine and holy books out into the cemeteries where the faithful were buried and began worshiping *with* them. Then they did something even more extraordinary. In the sixth century they began moving their dead inside the walls and onto sacred ground where they could be nestled around the church, and some of them they moved *into* the church. They began treating the dead saints as friends, invisible companions, and teachers.

Just consider their credentials. Because they are eternal, they are more like God than like us. They are present to the living God night and day in a realm where there is no night and there is no day. In his *Confessions*, Augustine says they live in a zone where the date is always "Today." For poor time-kept creatures like us, they offer the eternal perspective. They provide little tutorials on how to live eternally amidst the challenges of time. They make it easier for us to live as though Jesus Christ is risen from the dead. Which he is.

These faithful people are not figures painted in plaster or carved into pulpits. Before they are heroes, they are friends. They are our companions and teachers of another realm. And in teaching us how to die, they show us what real life is all about.

30

THE ROCK AND THE RIVER

There is a river whose streams make glad the city of God.
—PSALM 46

One of the oldest metaphors for the Bible is *liber et speculum*, the book and the mirror. Look into the book and, presto, it becomes a mirror. In the book you can see ancient Israel, the prophets, the ministry of Jesus, Peter, Paul, and who knows what else. Read Psalm 46, and you meet an ancient victim of violence and war, whose only hope is that Yahweh will destroy the ancient equivalents of land mines and assault rifles.

Keep looking. You may have to squint a little, and when you do, you will see yourself—as you are, threatened by the trials of this life and the dangers of our own age. And, as if by magic, you will see yourself as you hope to be, free from every pestilence and fear. The mirror of God's Word never lies. Not about God, not about us.

Tonight, our mirror is the music of Johann Sebastian Bach. In it we hear the turbulence of our fears and the serenity of our faith in Jesus Christ. His Cantata no. 80, the "Mighty Fortress" cantata, sets God's Word and our faith to music. A great scribbler in the margins of his compositions, he wrote at the bottom of his cantatas *Soli deo Gloria*, to God alone the glory. He made notes in his Bible too. Beside 2 Chronicles 5, which tells how the ark of the covenant was brought into the newly completed temple accompanied by harps, lyres, cymbals, and twenty priests on trumpet, he wrote, "NB, where

there is devotional music, God with his grace is always present." Bach
was right. Tonight, as the sun is setting and the music rising and the
first word of the homily has hardly been spoken, the glory of God
already fills our temple.

The great Bach scholar John Eliot Gardner writes that Bach's genius is such that "his cantatas appear to escape their historical and
liturgical confinement and reach out to us today."

To which I would add, "Just as the psalms do."

Perhaps it takes a guarded and wary people like us to notice how
security conscious the psalms are. In them, security has many names—
my rock, my hiding place, my shelter, my fortress, my tower, even "He
will cover you with his feathers" (see *March of the Penguins*).

We can appreciate why Luther chose Psalm 46 as his battle hymn
for, having publicly taken sides with the Word of God, he was feeling
a bit exposed. The Holy Roman Empire was trembling with conflict.
Writing to Pope Leo X, he says, I am "living among the monsters
of this age . . . with whom I am waging war." In this light, we can
understand why on September 14, 2001, the vast congregation in
the National Cathedral sang "A Mighty Fortress Is Our God." The
psalmist's image of God as a fortress is a mirror to our own sense of
siege and our growing realization that there are no safe zones in an
open society. It addresses our obsession with unlisted numbers, ever-
changing security codes, gated communities, surveillance cameras,
scanners, guns, and our fear of every skin shade and dress option
but our own.

The fear is not new to us. When I was a boy, our grade school
held nuclear attack drills. Sometimes we were taken to the school
basement. Other times we were told to crawl under our desks, the
thought being that there's nothing like a sturdy pine school desk to
ward off a hydrogen bomb. Several weeks ago, one of our grandsons
told me his middle school had recently gone into lockdown. Apparently, someone was firing a gun a few blocks from the school. "What
happens in a lockdown?" I asked. "We try to make the room look
empty." "How?" I asked. "We crawl under our desks."

Even in quieter times, we relied on our special places of refuge. Our shelters were the tree house from which you could pull up the ladder; the sewing room, which offered sanctuary from the laundry; the workshop in the garage where you could putter away your worries. For me, it was the basketball hoop on the driveway, where you could jump-shoot your troubles away.

There are shelters in the mind, too, where we indulge our fantasies of defeating our competitors or—with the help of a superior military, two oceans, and a wall—of insulating the homeland from every foreign enemy. But the mirror doesn't lie. Only God can shatter the weapons of war, including our own; only God can stop life's disintegration feared by the psalmist, and now by us.

The psalmist says, "We will not fear though the earth should change." As we age, the ground begins to shift beneath our feet. People we love are disappearing at an alarming rate. Strategies that once got us through are no longer working. The only permanent reality we know is change. At the health clinic, after you've been asked your date of birth, the next question is, "Have you fallen recently?" And you begin to tell the intake person more than she wants to know: "Well, yes and no. Maybe not physically, but I could use something solid to lean on. There are times I feel that I *could* fall." Thank you, please take a seat. Someone will call you.

Our God, though, is not a crutch or a fortress, for that matter, but a loving Father. Or in Isaiah's image, a nursing Mother, who is always there. Lean on me, child.

That brings me to the tenderest part of this psalm. "Be still and know that I am God." The psalm invites us to become fluent in silence. What could be sweeter? There is a time to speak and a time to be still and to let the promises of God speak for themselves. When I hear *Be still*, I don't hear a rebuke like "shut up," but rather the gift of peace to those who are beset with the multiple anxieties of our age. Not "be quiet" but "Don't be afraid." You don't have to talk. You don't have to figure all this out. In memory units around the world, it speaks to all who have come to the end of words.

The day must come for each of us when we quit projecting our own voice into the sound and fury of debate and begin to listen, really listen, to other voices. And if you are just still enough, you can hear the one essential voice, the way a frightened child hears the reassuring voice of its mother or father. It's what the rabbis meant by insisting that God gave not only the words in the Torah but the white spaces between the words. Which I take to mean that God is the author of silence as well as talk.

Bach is frequently called the fifth evangelist. I prefer to think of him as the second psalmist. Listen to the big fortress-like chords that advertise the strength of God, but also to the twists, turns, and the repeats of a river dancing its way through the music. He knows God and he knows the human heart.

Psalm 46 and Cantata no. 80 show the second, less familiar side of God. Faith isn't always a matter of "Here I Stand," but "Here I Swim"—in treacherous currents deeper than I suspected and in circumstances I cannot master.

> There is a river whose streams
> shall make glad the city of God,
> the holy habitation of the Most High;
> God is in the midst of her.
> God shall help her and that right early.

God no longer lives exclusively at the top of the tower. In the healing ministry, death, and resurrection of Jesus, God descends and joins us in the surprising eddies and dangerous currents of life. A river can take us to places we never intended to go. It can overflow its banks, destroy levees, and bring devastation. But in the Bible, the river is almost always a life-giving force. "Go bathe in the river," Jesus tells the afflicted.

There is a river. God is more than our personal fortress against the attacks of others. One is always playing defense in a fortress. A fortress is nice, but it's no place to live. You can't raise a child in a fortress.

You probably won't find love in a fortress. If the life of faith is only a fortress, we are a fortress too easily breached and in too many places: when we are young, we are breached by inexperience; in middle age we are breached by pride; and in old age—just breached.

God is not only "Fort God" but the God who moves with us in these treacherous currents, who appears in the needs of the stranger, in small acts of faithfulness, and in our own suffering. Rejoice in the river. A river runs through us. In all its joys and profound suffering, God flows with us, the way Bach's music dances and twists like a river through the mighty affirmations of the whole cantata.

It was as if by coming *down* God was reconceiving what it means to be "God." The Lord Jesus left the fortress and ventured into the dangers and uncertainties of the river. At his crucifixion he said, "Don't you think I could call on my Father and he would send seventy legions of angels." But he never asked, and they never came. At baptism we practice the same vulnerability. We make the sign of his cross, and say (often to a defenseless child), "The Lord preserve your going out and your coming in from this time forth and forevermore." And then we let the baby go, as if releasing a bottle into open water. We abandon those we love, even as we have been abandoned, to a greater love.

We don't have to choose between the rock and the river. Our God is both.

A fortress in time of trouble.

And a river to carry us home.

31

THE VIEW FROM THE DITCH

*"Which of these three, do you think, was a neighbor to the
man who fell into the hands of the robbers?"*

—LUKE 10:25–37

So, once again this week, the American flag flies at half-staff, and the
old question about our "national character" has arisen for debate. Six
people are dead, including a nine-year-old child. A congresswoman
lies gravely wounded, shot at point-blank range with a semiauto-
matic pistol. What continuing madness is this? Where does all this
hatred come from? Why this violence? Why these guns? We have
been schooled in our rights, but what are our responsibilities to one
another? And who are we as part of this community of Christ? What
is our vision of the kingdom?

On the night before he was assassinated, Martin Luther King Jr.
was wrestling with many of the same questions. He was making a
speech in Memphis, recounting how he had become involved in a
local dispute involving sanitation workers. What did a Nobel lau-
reate have to do with striking garbagemen? His closest aides asked
the same question and reminded him that he had more important
things to do. Memphis was not a strategic city. The sanitation workers were not attractive victims like the children of Birmingham or the
voters of Selma. As King spoke that night, a powerful storm rumbled
through Memphis, and his speech was punctuated by claps of thun-
der, as if to say, "Listen, this is important!"

The historian Taylor Branch tells the backstory. Neighborhood residents had objected to the sanitation workers' practice of eating lunch and "picnicking" (as they called it) outside the trucks. The workers were therefore instructed to eat in the truck, but the cab of a truck would not accommodate a crew of four. One rainy afternoon, two of the workers crawled into the compactor on the back of the truck to eat their sandwiches. Something shorted in the electrical gear, the system engaged, and the two workers were compacted, like garbage. It's no wonder that later, when their colleagues went on strike, many wore signs that read, "I am a man."

On that stormy night King preaches a sermon on the Good Samaritan. A certain man was making a dangerous journey from Jerusalem to Jericho when he fell among thieves and was robbed, thrown in a ditch and left for dead. In his speech King declares that today the man in the ditch is the sanitation worker. He asks us to imagine why two religious professionals, the priest and Levite, chose not to stop and help. Perhaps, he says, it was because they were late for a meeting of the Jericho Improvement Association, or perhaps they were more concerned with the law that forbids defilement. Or maybe they were just afraid. You stop on a road like that, and *you* may be the next victim. You open your home to the wrong people, and they will rob you blind. A church that stands up for the wrong cause may find itself in the ditch. In his speech, King says even honorable people ask, "What will happen to me if I stop?"

"What will happen to me?" It's a familiar question, the question of self-interest. Among politicians of both parties, it takes the form of the familiar mantra "the middle class." If we provide benefits to the poor, in terms of health care, better education, or other protections, what will be the effect on the middle class? Not "What will happen to the poor if they are not cared for?"—which is the prophets' question throughout Israel's Scripture—but "What will happen to us?" "We are the ones who are suffering," my affluent friend says about the tax laws. Likewise, the church asks, "If we focus our ministry on the needy, if we try to make a budget worthy of the prophets, what will happen to us as an institution?" The more urgent question, King said in his last speech, is not "What will happen to me if I *do* stop?" but "What will happen to *them* if I *do not*?" For King, despite his staff's warnings, Memphis was not a detour from a more important destination. It *was* his destination—and his destiny.

King preached the parable of the Good Samaritan a lot. I guess all preachers do. And, like all preachers, he told it with a variety of emphases. His entire ministry contributed to another, more profound approach to the Good Samaritan. In that version the person in the ditch is not the sanitation worker, or the black man, or the poor woman, or the immigrant. *America* is in the ditch. It is America and the American church, as he often said, that has lost its way on a dangerous road. It has been stripped of its compassion and fundamental commitments and is in desperate need of rescue. It is America, he said, that wastes so much of its resources on war that it has nothing left for the poor. It is America that continues to make absolute distinctions between white and black, citizen and immigrant, rich and poor, and thereby enables an environment of hate and division. And it is the American church, he wrote in his famous "Letter from Birmingham Jail," that preaches personal morality to the skies but on the weightier issues of justice and mercy remains silent.

If America is in the ditch, who is this Samaritan? Jesus himself gives the answer. The Good Samaritan is the foreigner, the outsider, the "other." The Good Samaritan is the last person you want to see when you're in need of a helping hand. In Jesus's day, Samaritans were hated traitors to Israel and renegades to the true religion. On one occasion Jesus had to dissuade his disciples from calling down fire on a Samaritan village. In his day, King identified the Good Samaritan with the black civil rights movement. By its willingness to suffer and work for change nonviolently, this movement would pull America (and the American church with it) out of the ditch.

In this approach to the story, the question is not "Are you willing to stop and help?" but "Are you *ready* to be rescued?" When Jesus first told the story, his hearers would have instinctively identified not with the helper but with the person in need of help, the man in the ditch. He is the ordinary Jewish layperson on an ordinary journey who winds up in the ditch. Everyone can relate to that. Jesus seems to be saying, "Don't you see? It's somebody like you. Why, it *is* you! You are the unfortunate man or woman in the ditch. You are the church in the ditch, the nation in the ditch." Now for the hard part: Are you willing to concede that people *unlike you* may prove redemptive *for you*? *Can you imagine that their fortitude in suffering and nonviolent resistance may be instructive for you?*

From whom are you willing to accept help? From whom are you willing to learn?*

At this point in our history, you could say we've tried our share of salvations. We've tried unbridled expressions of rage, we've tried conspiracy theories, we've tried rights without responsibilities; we've armed ourselves to the teeth.

And we are not saved.

To whom shall we turn? Are there any *other* options out there? In his day, King made a controversial proposal. Guided by Jesus's ministry and death, he suggested that we try to love one another. It's hard to imagine how the idea of love could be controversial, especially coming from a preacher. But he made it *very* controversial, because he took love out from under the sacred canopy of the pulpit, where it's the safe, expected word, and injected it into the realm of social conflict and public policy.

He even had a controversial name for his method. He called it "the weapon of love." "What's love got to do with it?" his more militant opponents asked. "We're tired of this love-your-neighbor business. Look where it got us."

"How can love be a weapon?" the theologians asked. A fist is a weapon. A gun is a weapon. If you believe love is limited to personal and family relationships, you will agree with them. But King believed

---

* With thanks for the literary and theological insights of Robert W. Funk and John Dominic Crossan.

that when people work together in concert with their faith, their nonviolent resistance to dogs and tear gas represents another version of God's self-giving love.

He was always speaking about love in all the wrong places: on the streets, in pool halls, in city halls, in fire-bombed churches, even on this campus (in a still-segregated university). When he might have been talking about revenge, he spoke of reconciliation.

After his parsonage was bombed, he wrote, "We shall match your capacity to inflict suffering by our capacity to endure suffering. We will meet your physical force with soul force. Do to us what you will and we will still love you. We cannot in all good conscience obey your unjust laws and abide by the unjust system ... so throw us in jail, and we will still love you. Bomb our homes and threaten our children and, as difficult as it is, we will still love you."

Much has been written lately about what a savvy political operator King was, but these words do not sound "savvy" to me, any more than a crucifixion is a shrewd method of getting your way in the world.

The story of the Good Samaritan is really two separate stories. Viewed from the road, it's a story of encouragement to help those who are lost and hurting, the way King did in Memphis, the way Jesus did throughout his ministry, the way we do in our better moments.

Viewed from the ditch, however, where all of us have been at one time or another, the same story takes on a different character. It asks an even more profound question: Despite your own privileged education, wealth, and status, do you understand how God might be using someone or something you never imagined to teach you a new and better way of life?

When God decided to redeem humanity, he sent someone we were not expecting. He sent a man named Jesus, whose teaching challenged the complacency of our religious categories and whose death scandalized our ideas of greatness. He was the one of whom Isaiah said, "He had no form or majesty that we should look at him, and no beauty that we should desire him." The human race asked for help. And God sent redemption in the form of a crucified Jew/ Samaritan. An outsider. Is this a helping hand you can accept? Is this a mercy you can receive?

Yes, it's a dangerous road, this winding road from Jerusalem to Jericho, and anyone can wind up in the ditch. Even you.

How dangerous? This road will change your life, because on this road old enemies become neighbors—then friends.

How dangerous? It will cause you, of all people, to lift your arms to a crucified Teller of Tales.

32

HEARTS SET FREE

*But now, apart from law, the righteousness of God has been
disclosed, and is attested by the law and the prophets, the
righteousness of God through faith in Jesus Christ for all
who believe.*

—ROMANS 3:19–28

It was one of those dialogues that can only take place in a university.
In a small seminar on psychiatry and religion, faculty members from
the medical school and the divinity school are sitting on opposite
sides of a table discussing how medicine and religion can heal the
human spirit. The divinity-school speaker briefly outlines the life-
giving elements of the Christian message. When he finishes, one
of the young residents replies, "I grew up in a Christian home, and
I never experienced the healing of the spirit you talk about or what
you have repeatedly called 'grace,' but only 'do this, do that,' or 'don't
do this, don't do that.'" For a moment the conversation is suspended
in midair. It is painfully clear (to me) that at the mention of "gospel,"
the young man hears "law," and that the only Christian home he has
ever known is a house of boundaries. I also note a small worm of
self-satisfaction in my diagnosis of his condition.

Then, to amplify his point he adds, "I have a patient who thinks
she has sinned against God and that God knows what she is thinking.
Can you imagine that?" O dear, I *can* imagine that (as I quietly take
stock of my own mental health), but I keep my mouth shut. I recall

Augustine's metaphor for the soul as a house that needs cleaning. Are there rooms in my house I would rather my Lord didn't visit? he asks. Absolutely. Then, relenting, he invites the Lord to enter all the rooms and to view the thoughts and secrets of his heart. The implication of the young man's response is obvious to everyone in the room. Christianity is an unhealthy religion. It creates burdens of guilt where none should exist. Even though he grew up in a Christian home, the only Christianity he has experienced is bondage, from which he is now free at last.

I suppose answers could be given and defenses made. But before one gets defensive, one must recognize that the young doctor has a point. We owe it to him to listen carefully to his testimony. Christians are at home with guilt. The message of God's goodness comes with an inevitable negative. Shakespeare's Othello says of his opponent, "He hath a daily beauty in his life that makes me ugly." The notion of *ugly* rears its head whenever one speaks of the beauty of God. What does God's beauty make *me*? When I was a boy, our weekly confession began, "I, a poor miserable sinner..." In the classic allegory *Pilgrim's Progress*, one of the things that makes Christian's journey toward the heavenly city so hard is the suitcase filled with sins he carries on his back.

So, the accuser points his finger at us and says, "You Christians really love to wallow in your own sins. You make your confession every week, but do you *hear* the absolution—and live it? Do you really hear the voice of God when your pastor says, 'I declare to you the entire forgiveness of all your sins?' "

The religious movement we call the Reformation began with a man who, finally, after much pain, *got* the absolution. When the word of grace made contact with this tinderbox of a soul named Martin Luther, it set off such a conflagration that we really should not call it a reformation but a revolution in our understanding of God.

The revolution did not begin on October 31, 1517, with the actions of a rebellious monk. The original revolution is the gospel of Jesus Christ that sets us free from the power of sin, the curse of the law, and the finality of death. It enters our atmosphere like an uncharted meteor. Perhaps you've said about someone you thought you knew, "Well, that's a side of him/her I've never seen before." The supervisor who is invariably gruff or distant exercises unexpected compassion, and all we can say is, "Who saw that coming?" The gospel reveals a side of God (which is the *heart* of God) that not even the wisest philosophers or theologians saw coming. Just when you are expecting a No!, or at best a Maybe, there is, as Luther exclaims in one of his sermons, "a *Yes* in the heart of God!"

Paul calls such generosity the *righteousness* of God, which is often translated the *justice* of God. It's not a virtue or a quality easily translated. It doesn't help to look it up in a dictionary. When I try to understand righteousness, it's enough for me to think of it as God's very *self*.

How does one make contact with God's very self? Since Luther taught the church how to read the Bible, it's not surprising that when we want to learn more about the gospel, we consult the New Testament. And when we do that, we realize that the New Testament is a chronicle of one crisis after another. Which is to say, it looks an awful lot like our lives: someone is sick, someone is dying, someone is dead, someone is grieving, someone is possessed, someone is angry; someone is guilty, a church is divided, a boy is lost in the far country.

Luther had a word for these multiple crises that crack open our lives and leave us raw and exposed. He said, God comes to us by means of *Anfechtung*. *Anfechtung* is the ugly German word for struggle, testing, or turmoil. It is Jacob wrestling with the angel; it's Jeremiah plagued by self-doubt; it's the anonymous man in the Gospels confessing (while his son is writhing in the throes of a seizure), "Lord, I believe; help my unbelief." It is Jesus on the cross, crying out, "My God, my God, why have you forsaken me?"

"The more I want Him—the less I am wanted . . . there is that separation—that terrible emptiness, that feeling of the absence of God." These are not the words of Luther but of another troubled soul, Mother Teresa of Calcutta—*Saint* Teresa. They remind us of how we Christians sometimes struggle to know the God who lives on the dark side of the moon, cloaked in the mystery of simply "being God," who is darkness and not light. Luther made the beginner's mistake of trying to get to know God where God is hardest to know, where God does not *want* to be known, that is, in God's moral perfection. Luther's attempt to do just that proved to be a disaster.

When we read the life stories of men and women of faith, we can't help but be surprised by how many profess to have loved God *before* they found Jesus. But not Luther. In a brief memoir written the year before he died, he confesses the opposite: "I did not love, yes, I hated the righteous God who punished sinners, and secretly, if not blasphemously, I was angry with God." He remembers nothing but rage and blasphemy until, by the mercy of God, he learns from Paul that the righteousness of God comes only as a gift with no strings attached. In a phrase many mainline Christians seem to have forgotten, he adds, "Here I felt that I was altogether *born again* and had entered paradise itself through open gates."

There are two kinds of righteousness.

One form of righteousness is so pure and holy that it cannot stand to be touched by anything less than itself. That is the righteousness of the prude. It is a moral perfection to which everything and everyone else is a pollutant. It's bad enough to hang around with *people* who think like that. We can't survive a *God* like that.

A second form of righteousness is so pure and holy that it cannot help but share its goodness with others. That is the righteousness of the divine lover. Even if you've been brought up to believe that God's righteousness is of the first variety, once you get to know Jesus, you know that God is a giver, not a hoarder, of love.

If love is a gift, it means that we are "justified"—another of Paul's favorite words—or made right in God's sight. If everything is a gift, Paul asks defiantly, "what becomes of our boasting?"

I remember the city-wide Reformation festivals of yore: the chartered buses filled with ardent Lutherans from surrounding counties and southern Illinois, the massed choirs, the fiery sermons on "grace,"

the denunciations of the Catholics and their mistakes. Our St. Louis
Cardinals never won a pennant in those days, but we always had
Reformation Day. To a twelve-year old boy, it was wonderful.

"What has become of our boasting?"

Our boasting took the form of our own purity, which we had
inherited from our ancestors but without going through their *Anfechtung*, their struggle. *We* had never stood condemned by the law.
We had not wrestled with God or been sifted by Satan, as Luther and
others had. We were mere inheritors.

Isaac Watts wrote, "Forbid it, Lord, that I should boast, / save in
the death of Christ my God!" The old boasting continues but in new
forms. When hallowed slogans like *grace alone* or *faith alone* become
an excuse for anti-Judaism or anti-Semitism, as has happened in our
own church, then we have fumbled the gift and lost it. There are those
who boast in traits over which they had no control: the whiteness
of their skin, their European heritage, their gentile (= Christian)
identity, their straight sexual orientation. When racial supremacists,
anti-Semites, or homophobes make their noxious claims, they are
not just pumping their fists in the air. They are sinning against the
Gift. If I claim to be *right* because I am a straight, white, gentile, male
American—I am not *right*.

How to let go of this stuff that Paul calls "refuse" or what trans-
lators politely term "dung"? He shows us how to let go: "One
thing I do, forgetting what lies behind, straining toward what lies
ahead, I press on to the prize of the upward call of God in Christ
Jesus." I am remembering the title of a fine book about Paul by F. F.
Bruce, probably because it represents what I desperately want for
myself and for you as well: *Paul: Apostle of the Heart Set Free*.

When Garrison Keillor pokes fun at Minnesota and its Lutheran
state church, saying, "the weather is terrible and the theology is
enough to break a person's heart," he's got it wrong. Grace doesn't
break hearts; it sets them free. When you live out of the Gift, you are
free to live for others the way God is free to love us. The shackles are
off. For the first time in your life, you're traveling without luggage.

The freedom of the gospel is not an institution, but an *intuition*, which in every generation and in every community produces a creative *witness* to the grace of God.

In his memoir *A Grief Observed*, C. S. Lewis remembers that when his wife died, he did not ask, is there a God, but "what kind of God" do I have? It is a question born of grief, loneliness, and doubt. It was Luther's question too.

His answer is worth hearing. There's only one way to know, he said. Nature gives a mixed message. You can look at the grandeur of nature but also its ferocity. The wisdom of philosophy may help a little, but it offers no redemptive story. Even when we examine ourselves and sift through our own feelings and dreams, the picture is far from clear. A disciple begged Jesus, "Lord, show us the Father." Luther said, only look at the cross. There you see God's truest self. If you want a picture of the very being of God, look at the cross. That's the side of God (which is really the *heart* of God) that makes all the difference.

In a world in which gracelessness is the norm and grace the exception, where the rhetoric of hate and the practice of greed go hand in hand; where white supremacy mocks the supremacy of the Most High and the dignity of all human beings; where so many know the price of everything but the value of nothing—someone needs to tell the truth about Jesus. We are finished with massive Reformation carnivals (at least I am), but we will never lack for opportunities to stand up for Christ's gospel. For the best liberators are those who have been liberated. The best lovers are those who know what it is to be loved. The best forgivers are those whose sins have been forgiven. We are the people who have laid our backpacks down in order to stand up with others.

We are not defending the ancient fortress anymore but witnessing to the righteousness of God in whatever test is set before us. Then, by the grace of God and in the company of all who make the good confession, we will take our place in the Fellowship of Hearts Set Free.

33

THE WIDOW'S MIGHT

"Truly I tell you, this poor widow has put in more than all those who are contributing to the treasury. For all of them have contributed out of their abundance; but she out of her poverty has put in everything she had, all she had to live on."

—MARK 12:41–13:2

You know her, but not very well. For years now she's been alone. No one seems to remember her not being a solitary figure. She has no one to look after her, do her shopping, fight her battles for her. She receives a social security check every month and not one penny more. From that she gets rent, food, utilities, used clothing, bus fare, newspaper, entertainment, which amounts to little more than the electricity needed to generate *Wheel of Fortune*—and church. At church she is known for her acts of kindness, which in their generosity are well out of proportion to her modest means. She is not known at church for the size of her financial offerings. In fact, when the plate is passed, her expression often becomes one of disappointment. She gives her offering quickly and averts her eyes from those of the usher.

She doesn't sit on the church council or the board of finance. The minister does not confer with her on matters of importance. When her church finally builds the great bell tower, it will not be named in her honor. But then, she doesn't require a monument, not even a marble headstone when she dies, because she has already been memorialized in one small story.

Mark's Gospel is like an enormous fresco one would expect to see in an Italian church, with exciting and dramatic scenes taken from the ministry of Jesus. But if you aren't careful, you'll miss this bent shape placing her two lepta—hay-pennies—into the grand trumpet-shaped receptacle in the outer court of the temple. And you'll miss the small circle of men observing her from the shadows. She seems such an insignificant detail in the grand design.

Her social insignificance is accentuated by the presence of other, more important people mentioned by Jesus:

> Beware of the scribes—*read*: theological lawyers—who like to walk around in long robes, and to be greeted with respect in the market-places—"*Good morning, counselor*"—and to have the best seats in the synagogues and places of honor at banquets!—"*Your usual table, judge?*"—They devour widows' houses and for the sake of appearance say long prayers.

Added to her tiny social status, the old woman is physically dwarfed by the surrounding buildings. The physical backdrop of this story makes her look small: "And as Jesus came out of the temple, one of his disciples said to him, 'Look, Teacher, what wonderful stones and what wonderful buildings!' And Jesus said, 'Do you see these great buildings? There will not be left here one stone upon another that will not be thrown down.'"

So, there she is, the middle panel of three scenes in the temple, squeezed between the powerful lawyers and the magnificent buildings. A nobody.

It would be a shame to overlook the widow, because in her one can see a fragile emblem of the kingdom of God. In a world preoccupied with bigger things, she is easy to miss. But if God (and not the devil) is really in the details, then she takes her place beside a poor child in a manger, the paralytic at the pool, and the beggar on our block. Which is to say that in God's way of being in the world—his secret rule—she counts for everything. In God's ledger, she is the biggest giver.

Jesus isn't merely saying, "Yes, my generous Father will even make room for an insignificant nobody like this widow," as if she were an exception. No, that would make her a mere ornament on God's Christmas tree. The woman belongs at the center because she is totally dependent on God and out of her dependence gives everything.

The philosopher Kierkegaard tells a parable called "The Swindler and the Widow's Mite," in which the widow wraps her two pennies in a little cloth before she goes up to the temple to make her offering. On her way, a flimflam artist tricks her into exchanging her cloth for an empty one, with the result that, unbeknownst to her, she places an empty handkerchief in the temple treasury. Kierkegaard asks, "I wonder if Christ would not still have said what he said of her, that 'she gave more than all the rich?'"

In the first church I served, my predecessor had been a missionary in India. He had sacrificed a great deal over many years and had been rewarded with a poor, out-of-the-way parish in a tiny farming community. By the end of his life, he and his wife were living on practically nothing. These were not prosperous years for farmers or the clergy. When I studied the church's budget, however, I made a surprising discovery. The church that one might have expected to be insulated from the world was giving half of its income to missions every year.

One day I asked the treasurer, "How is it that we give away so much money?"

"Oh, that would be Pastor Martin," he said.

"What did Pastor Martin have to do with it?"

"Well, every month when I would give him his paycheck, he would ask me the same question—always on the QT, mind you—'have you paid our mission pledge?' And I would have to say, 'No, we're running behind.' And he says to me, 'Just take it out of my check. First pay missions, always. Then pay me. Understand?'" The treasurer added, "You know, this is a small town, what he was doing gradually got around. And it changed us."

In that same congregation we had a little girl named Amy, confined to a wheelchair from an early age. One day a famous faith healer came to the big city across the river. Lots of people from our county were intent on going to see her, including Amy. It seemed indelicate to mention healing, but in my own pastoral way I cautioned Amy against expecting too much. Maybe she should be satisfied with the bus ride, the massed choirs, and a good worship experience. She smiled at me sweetly from her wheelchair and replied, "Oh no, Pastor, I'm going for the cure."

It didn't happen. But I needn't have worried that she would become disillusioned or bitter, for the next time I saw her she was as cheerful as ever. It was Amy's lesson to us all. The act of trusting God is a replenishing activity, like planting a garden or helping a neighbor. No need to hold back your best for a more suitable occasion. When you give of yourself fully, there will always be more to give. Faith makes faith. With our cost/benefit mentality, we don't always see it that way. But God does. What the world counts as *little* God receives as *all*. What the rich compute as *nothing* God celebrates as *everything* (on Pastor Martin and Amy, see my *Open Secrets: A Memoir of Faith and Discovery*).

In fact, I think I can see the Lord in the shadows now, no longer standing with his disciples beside a pillar in the temple, but with his arms folded, observing us from beneath the balcony of a country church, still astonished by the lives of his saints.

"I tell you, he gave more than the whole congregation put together," he says.

"She gave me all the faith she had. She held nothing back. When the splendor of this world has been forgotten, I tell you, she will be remembered." By God.

Public Callings

34

THERE WILL BE BLOOD

There is no distinction, since all have sinned and fall short
of the glory of God; they are now justified by his grace as a
gift, through the redemption that is in Christ Jesus, whom
God put forward as a sacrifice of atonement by his blood.

—ROMANS 3:21–28; 5:12–17

Today is "Cross Day" in the Divinity School. It's that time of year
when we recognize the graduates among us. It's happening all over
our community and on campuses everywhere. After a recent basketball game, the spectators cheered as first the graduating players and
then the cheerleaders were brought out to take a bow. Each of the
cheerleaders was given a bouquet of roses.

Today, dear graduates, it is your day. And in recognition of your
achievements, we will present each of you with—a cross, the universal symbol of shame, suffering, and degradation.

Congrats.

Admittedly, Paul's words in our text might not be appropriate
on a day like today, especially if we were about to present you with a
basket of fruit or a bouquet of roses. But Romans 3 matches up well
with the gift of a cross.

Over the years I've listened to quite a few reasons why students do
not *like* the apostle Paul and would prefer to avoid roughly one-third
of the New Testament canon: Paul is too doctrinaire; too difficult
to follow; too sure of himself. He is too obsessed with the cross; too
masculine in his orientation. He doesn't tell enough stories.

But let me say, Paul will work for you, especially those of you who care deeply about ministry. For if you were to look up the word "mission" in a theological dictionary, it might well say "*See* Paul, apostle." If you were to look up "gospel," it might add "*See* Paul, prisoner for." If you were to look up "reconciliation," it would say "*See* Romans, letter to." Like you, Paul has been transformed by his experience of the grace of God, and, like you, he has been formed and disciplined for ministry. With this letter he is on his way to a new field placement. He's never been to Rome, but he knows there are Romans out there, and he's determined to be their pastor.

What he eventually discovers is a divided community. Under the emperor Claudius, Jewish followers of Jesus had been expelled from Rome as troublemakers. In their absence, gentile believers have assumed positions of leadership in the new movement. But now, under Nero, the Jews are being allowed to return, creating, shall we say, a *complex* social and religious situation in the one, holy, Christian, and apostolic church. Each group is defining itself and claiming its privileges by means of *difference* rather than by a common bond of faith.

Add to the mix the loud voices of leaders who specialize in turning outsiders into enemies, who magnify *difference* to their own advantage, and you have a recipe for a broken church—and, we might add, a broken country: "This is how I know who *I* am, by looking carefully at *you* and memorizing our differences. You are a man; I am a woman. You are white; I am black. You are straight; I am gay. You are a liberal; I am a conservative. You are satisfied; I am outraged." Paul understands the complexities. He is a Jewish Christian himself. It's personal.

We are living in what he characterizes as dueling histories. One is a history of sin and death. It is a history marked by division, corruption, and injustice. Paul's name for this history is *Adam*. *Adam* is the sin that clings so closely. *Adam* is the past that sticks to us like chewing gum at the bottom of our shoe. As William Faulkner famously said, "The past isn't dead; it isn't even past." On this campus, we live in an Adamite community in which somebody can put up a symbolic noose in a public place or scrawl a hateful word on a wall, as happened just last week, and generate real pain throughout the whole body. One hateful gesture, one ugly word, and suddenly an entire history is exposed for all to see.

The second history is one of redemption. Paul simply calls this history *Jesus Christ*. That history was not lived in heaven—there is no history in heaven!—but in the neighborhoods, churches, synagogues, and courtrooms of *this* history. In Jesus, God touches every piece and place of our history and offers them redemption.

In Romans Paul is addressing two peoples who are convinced that their two distinct histories are unbridgeable. One says, in effect, "This is how I know I am a civilized human being, when I look at you, *Jew*, with your abject reliance on the law and your pride of chosenness." The other party might say, in effect, "This is how I know I am one of God's chosen people, when I look at you, *Goy*, the way you live, the way you prattle on about 'freedom'—and the unholy food you eat."

America also has its two histories: one, taking pride in its identity, resilience, legacy of suffering, and the beauty of its color and its music. The other, reflecting a different sort of pride, exemplified by such phrases as "Know yourself" or "Man is the measure of all things," boasting in its heritage of cultural dominance and its absence of color. Two histories—one black, another white: one church. It is the American typology, which includes other histories—Hispanic, Native American, Asian, and among these the multiple histories of regions, tribes, and nations. Other histories crowd the story, histories of the excluded: feminine, gay, queer, trans. So many histories involved in *Adam* and *Christ*—how are we united? Where shall we all meet?

Paul refuses to create a false history inhabited by superior and inferior players. Nor will he take refuge in his own privileged status as a Jew and a teacher. Everyone is a sinner, and from God's good heart everyone receives mercy. About his own people, the Jews, he says, "The gifts and call of God are irrevocable," just as an ironclad trust is irrevocable. To the gentiles he says, Israel's root is holy, which makes your branches golden. You are both made right but in a different order.

Paul is like the man with one foot on a banana peel and the other foot on a banana peel. He's looking for a place to stand. He's looking for a meeting place.

He finds it in the phrase "whom God put forward as a sacrifice of atonement by his blood." You may know that the text really says, "whom God put forward as a 'mercy seat' by his blood." The mercy seat was the cover or lid on the ark of the covenant that hid the tablets of the law from God's eyes. It was the place where once a year the blood of an animal was sprinkled on behalf of a sinful people. Paul has found a new place, a new mercy seat, which isn't a place at all but a person.

Then, as if to seal the deal, he chooses the most universal and (to us) the most repulsive metaphor at his disposal—the blood. The notion of blood is so primitive, so redolent of the slaughter stone, so theologically unacceptable—so *Paul*.

But "by his blood" is not as primitive as you might think. Denigrate the blood to the scientists and technicians across campus in hematology, who spend their day analyzing the properties of the blood. Tell it to Shakespeare, whose character Shylock the Jew claims blood as the infallible sign of his humanity.

We read our blood like a tell-all biography. What do you want to know about yourself? Just ask the blood: The blood says, "I see cardiac enzymes—you've had a heart attack. I see cholesterol, diabetes, anemia, leukemia, HIV virus." Sometimes the blood says, "Congratulations. You're pregnant!" At other times, "No, you're not the father." The war of white and red rages in our bodies. It is the river of our mortal nature. The blood done signed your name—and mine.

A trauma nurse told me this story. One day a little boy was brought into the ER, an eight-year-old, who had been caught in the crossfire of a shooting and grievously wounded. He was rushed to surgery, where surgeons, nurses, and technicians fought valiantly through the night to save his life. It was a long, hard fight, but in the end the boy died. Everyone in the operating theater was crushed. One of the surgeons asked my friend, "How many units did we give him?" She answered, "Forty-two." He said, "What a waste of good blood. All our work for nothing."

I wonder if God ever looks down on the carnage of our days and says, "What a waste of good blood. All my work for nothing." When God sees one child caught in a crossfire, to say nothing of the bad blood that flows this way and that among us all, I wonder if God ever says, "What a waste."

Abraham Lincoln saw the waste and shuddered at the thought of divine retribution in the blood, when in his magnificent Second Inaugural he said, "Every drop of blood drawn with the lash shall be paid by another drawn with the sword."

Ministry is a bloody business. Soon, many of you will see it most intimately. You will weep with those who weep and rage with those who rage—at the waste of it all.

There is one, however, whose blood is not wasted. Just one. It avails. In Jesus, God begins a new history that ends not in death but in life. God takes us past the retribution Lincoln feared to the reconciliation for which he prayed. You will steel yourself to the waste, and in the very face of it proclaim the victory of the one who was crucified and raised from the dead.

The Bible calls it good news. If consulted, I would have called it "terrible news," not terrible in the sense of "bad," but terrible in the sense of a profound and mysterious power that refuses to be wasted. The kind of power that took Jesus to the cross and caused the women at the tomb to flee terrified. This is the news that we have tried to share with you. We have not been ashamed to tell the whole bloody story of God's love.

Perhaps you can understand, then, why we award you a cross today, and not a bouquet.

35

Odd Job—An Encouragement

*Therefore, having this ministry by the mercy of God, we
do not lose heart.*

—2 CORINTHIANS 4:1

According to findings reported in the *Pulpit & Pew National Clergy
Survey*, most clergy are deeply satisfied with the pastoral ministry.
Seven out of ten report that they have never considered abandoning
their vocation. In other words, most pastors claim to have found
happiness in the ministry.

Why is this disturbing? Some of us in academia have made a decent living chronicling the malaise of our fellow clergy. For years
we've had our students read the appropriate literature, from *Elmer
Gantry* to *Wise Blood*, on the implicit assumption that these and
other portraits of slightly out-of-whack ministers accurately represent the norm of vocational misery among Protestant clergy. Indeed,
Flannery O'Connor's tormented Hazel Motes appears to have more
in common with the tormented apostle Paul than those, like us, who
have found happiness in ministry.

Take Paul. In 2 Corinthians Paul narrates his ministry as a con-
tinuous near-death experience, as if ministry consists of thousands of
minifunerals and mini-Easters, moments of truth, when this defeat
or that triumph puts the crucified and risen Lord right there with
him on the razor's edge of his calling.

"For while we live, we are always being given up to death for Jesus's sake, so that the life of Jesus may be made visible in our bodies . . . so death is at work in us, but life in you." Later, in a typical 110-word sentence, Paul is pushing the envelope of language as he throws out image after ecstatic image of hard times on the mission circuit: calamities, beatings, imprisonments, as unknown and yet well-known, when suddenly he blurts out, "as dying—and see—we live."

This is all very dramatic, but many ministers are weary with the long hours and emotional fatigue that come with the office and, understandably, are no longer thrilled with the cruciform metaphor for ministry. Paul's theology appears to provide a rationale for the victimization of the clergy, what years ago theologian Joseph Sittler called the "maceration"—that is, the slicing and dicing—of the minister.

And yet, what Paul really offers is an escape from the macerating criteria for evaluating the effectiveness of a ministry. He offers a conception of ministry that focuses on the goodness of the work itself and not its circumstances or outcomes. His dialectic of death and resurrection suggests a realism that transcends our language of happiness and unhappiness in ministry. Indeed, it forges a tool for critiquing our best notions of happy and unhappy, satisfied and dissatisfied, successful and unsuccessful.

Having *this* ministry—the phrase reminds us that this thing we are accustomed to measure, analyze, and discuss at conferences is a blazing fire that cannot be touched. It is a gift, as Paul says in Ephesians, a grace "given to me for you."

The question is, what *kind* of gift is ministry? It's the kind that requires hours and hours of assembly, the sort of gift that even as you are taking it out of the box, you know the hour will come when you will be very sorry to have received it. You know *exactly* what kind of gift it is when the *giver* says, "Here, this gift is for you. Try not to let it discourage you."

"Oh, all this heartache for little me—you really shouldn't have."

It's as if Paul understands that our truest heartaches, like his, derive not from the culture, the economy, or the political climate, but from the ministry itself. The heartaches are not *cured* by ministry, they are *caused* by ministry. Having this ministry is like having children. Yes, in some respects they are an answer to prayer, but they also stimulate many desperate prayers as well. And all the joy they bring into your life is sharpened by the possibilities of new pain.

The French have an expression for the inevitable fatigue and pain that come with honest work. When an apprentice gets hurt, or complains of being tired, his coworkers are apt to say, "It is the trade entering his body." Over time, something like this happens to ministers and other caregivers too. The effect is cumulative. When the baptism occurs in a neonatal intensive care unit, and the baby is not expected to live; when the opioid epidemic reaches into the heart of the congregation and takes its heartless toll, something of the "trade" enters the body and soul of the pastor. The sadness of the caregiver cannot be compared to the suffering experienced by loved ones or victims, but it is real and cannot be tempered by a posture of professionalism. No, this, too, is the ministry we have. It's why Paul says, don't lose heart.

This ministry is like love: it never ends. It never comes to the end of its rope. It never wrings its hands and says, "There's nothing more to be done." By its very nature it can never run out of material. Which means there can never be a "bad" time for ministry. Because the very conditions of its defeat only create the possibilities for its rebirth.

Can a war defeat ministry? No. War produces an occasion for the ministry of comfort and justice. Can conflicts over sexuality destroy ministry? From painful experience, we are tempted to say yes, but even Paul would say they elicit the ministry of reconciliation. Can death bring ministry to an end? No, as one of Georges Bernanos's characters in *The Diary of a Country Priest* says to the new priest, "Love is stronger than death—that stands within your books."

One Maundy Thursday afternoon I was in the checkout line at Target and ran into a recent graduate of the divinity school, a young Mennonite pastor and friend named Isaac. He was buying two large plastic tubs. "What's with the tubs?" I asked. "Oh," he said, "as I was putting the final touches on my homily this morning, I realized we have nothing to wash feet in tonight. Aren't they nice?"

I couldn't help but think, "What an odd job." From Greek exegesis in the morning, to Target in the afternoon, to the Great Thanksgiving in the assembly of God's people in the evening. What a great job.

There is something about *this* ministry that cannot be captured by sociologists and church growth experts. Which is why, I suspect, Paul refers to it elsewhere as a "secret." I stand with the seven in ten who will not renounce their vocation. I rejoice with any who are foolish enough to admit they are satisfied, even happy, in ministry, because they are either slightly daft or in on the secret. Because if you live in a world like ours, whose attitude toward ministry runs the secular gamut from *condescension* to *contempt*, you would have to be crazy to say "I love the ministry!"—unless you are in on the secret and have what Paul had. Unless you too have glimpsed its holiness and apprehended it for the gift that it is. Unless you too have experienced its hard-won joy.

36

THE KNOW-NOTHING PREACHER—
THE INSTALLATION OF AUSTIN MCIVER
"MACK" DENNIS

*When I came to you, brothers and sisters, I did not come
proclaiming the mystery of God to you in lofty words or
wisdom. For I decided to know nothing among you except
Jesus Christ, and him crucified.*

—1 CORINTHIANS 2:1–5

So, today, by the mercy of God, the dance begins in earnest. There's
no good word for this new relationship. Let's call it a divine tango
between two awkward partners, a congregation and its new pastor.
I don't know if Baptists are good dancers. I've heard not. I can assure
you that Lutherans are worse. How long will it take to find your own
rhythm on the dance floor? Who will lead? Who will follow? Or
will that be an issue? Better, how will you move together, with what
grace—or the lack of it? Whose toes will be stepped on first?

The text I've chosen from 1 Corinthians reflects one pastor's strategy for dancing. The apostle Paul is narrating his first steps. They
are surprising.

In our current political climate, we expect our candidates to lead
with their most obvious gifts. They tell us in no uncertain terms who
they are and what they will do to make us a great or responsible nation.
It's all about them. This is the most fundamental difference between
leadership in politics and leadership in the church. Paul would have

made a terrible candidate, because he first announces what he cannot or will not do. He will not package his gospel to suit the fancies of the market. In this he reminds us of John the Baptist, whose first word in the Gospels is a stirring announcement of who he is *not*. I am not Messiah. I am not the one who is to come. If Paul were seeking employment today, he might say, "If you are looking for technological know-how or social media savvy, keep looking. If it's a smooth communicator you have in mind, frankly, I'm told I can be a little rough around the edges. If you are waiting for a guitar player, he is not coming."

I am trying to imagine how we would react to a lawyer we consulted who said, "I've decided to disregard everything I learned at Harvard Law School." You might say, "But I chose you *because* you went to Harvard Law School. It's all about credentials." Or a surgeon who says, "You know, the finer points of cutting your flesh are not that interesting to me."

Paul arrives in Corinth vowing to eliminate from his ministry the very thing his congregation craved the most: "plausible words of wisdom." The word to flag is the word "plausible." If the apostle sounds a wee bit defensive (or arrogant), it's because the Corinthians, like us, lived by what sociologists call "plausibility structures." They are the furniture of our life and thought. They are the "truths" that don't have to make sense because we no longer question them.

It wasn't that many years ago when the so-called "Southern way of Life" and all it entailed in terms of race and privilege was so plausible to whites that it couldn't be questioned. It was "the way things are." And in a very different sense, that same way of life was so clear to blacks that it needed no explanation. There was a time when America's moral superiority to every nation on Earth was so obvious that no debate on the matter was required.

We hear plausible words of wisdom from the politicians who speak incessantly of protecting the middle class but never mention the poor. Why does this jar the Christian ear? Maybe it's because when Jesus entered the synagogue in Nazareth, he did not announce good news for the middle class. Paul, too, began his ministry by renouncing the very assumptions by which his parishioners understood themselves.

Is it any wonder that the average minister appears a bit *off-center*? A bit ill-equipped? She often seems lonely, perhaps because she is the designated ear to everyone's secrets. And yet, she is a public person— some would say a "professional"—with contacts, clients, parishioners, and friends galore. He is a private person who is never more at home than in his study with his books. Yet he is expected to be an extrovert who is cheerfully available to anyone at any time. In fact, he worries about being reduced to what theologian Stanley Hauerwas calls "a quivering mass of availability." He is a highly educated person, rich in degrees and loaded with debt, and yet he is always hewing to the One Thing that will make sense of all the schooling, long hours, and repetitive nature of the work.

The minister soon learns that to preach fifty sermons a year is not so much a matter of eloquence as it is endurance—both on her part and the congregation's. To befriend a gang of teenagers, to hold a wrinkled hand, to pray a lost soul into heaven—these are not highly complex actions. Even to tell the truth to people you have learned to love, hard as it is, is not complicated. But to *be* the person entrusted with such responsibilities—that is sheer gift.

Someone in Corinth may have asked Paul about his specialties in ministry. He doesn't have any. He has only the implausible word of the cross. "That's all I've got," he seems to say, like a poker player about to fold. But then he flashes his powerhouse of a hand: "We preach Christ crucified, a stumbling to Jews and folly to Greeks, but to those who are called, Christ, the power of God and the wisdom of God."

When he moves into his cheesy little office in Corinth with its low ceiling and whitewashed walls, he leaves his diplomas in his suitcase and hangs up a crucifix instead. Nothing else. It's not hard to imagine the whispers: Have you met our new Rev. Know-Nothing?

Paul lacks a philosophical or psychological foundation for his ministry. We have sought our footing in nature, in political power, in religious institutions and personal intuition. We have looked for it in every corner of the world except the little hill on which Jesus was crucified. If you are seeking the key to ministry, look no further. The cross contains a pastor's entire ministry and a congregation's entire mission.

Many years ago, a young woman accosted me after church and somewhat aggressively asked, "What does this church have to offer me?" It's not an unusual question, but it sometimes comes from a hidden place. I should have attended more closely to the questioner, the look in her eyes. If I had, maybe I would have answered with the one essential word she needed. But instead I recited the most attractive features of our "program." She looked at me with pained forbearance. "Well, that's nice, but I'm looking for a church that can help me die. Do you think your church is up to that—and what about you, Reverend?"

When Desmond Tutu handed in the final report of the Truth and Reconciliation Commission, he said, "We have looked the beast in the eye." When the church looks at the cross, it sees the very worst that human beings can do and the best that God can do. It's only human instinct to turn away from injustice, suffering, and death, and to pass by on the other side. But the cruciform pastor and the cruciform congregation do not flinch. Together, it is our vocation to turn *toward* those the world disregards and to minister with the fierceness and compassion of Christ's cross.

In the theater of ancient Greece, the actors' roles were designated by the wooden masks they wore. In the theater of our redemption, which is the church, both the minister and the congregation can feel trapped by their assigned masks. It can happen here too, if we are not brave. When Paul arrived for his meet-and-greet in Corinth, he showed up without a mask. Perhaps that's why he began his ministry with "fear and trembling." After all, a holy dance was about to begin. The mystery of our redemption was about to be unveiled.

Fear and trembling is not the same as "I'm always nervous when I meet new people." Or, "I'm hoping to make a good impression." Fear and trembling is Isaiah in the temple of the Lord. It is three women and an angel at the open tomb. It is the whole company of men and women who have wrestled with their vocation. It is the Spirit calling the dance at First Baptist Church with you, Mack Dennis, the new guy in town.

And so, dear friends and my beloved Dr. Know-Nothing, I wish you fear and a holy trembling before the majesty of ministry, and before the mercy of God and his son Jesus. Let the dance begin.

37

ORDERED TO THE MARK—THE ORDINATION OF ANDREW JACOB TUCKER

Then he said, "Let me go, for the day is breaking." But Jacob said, "I will not let you go, unless you bless me." So he said to him, "What is your name?" And he said, "Jacob."

—GENESIS 32:22–32

It's Friday night, and we are approaching the shank of the evening. A band named Barley Corn & Rye is setting up for a big evening of Irish music a few blocks away in Brightleaf Square. Over at the county stadium they're testing the Friday night lights for another great high school football game. Both the quarterback and the drum major are doing their stretches and rehearsing their moves. And here we are, in what we call the house of the Lord. We have lit our own Friday night lights and rounded up our own musicians to celebrate the launching of a new minister and a new ministry.

We celebrate it for two good reasons: ordination is a charism, that is, a gift of the Holy Spirit to the church. It does not duplicate a profession or reflect a career choice. It is one of the ways God orders—by ordaining—the ministry on earth. The old theologians had a rather clumsy phrase with which to describe the gift. They called it "office grace." So, before we talk about the considerable gifts you bring to this office, Andrew Jacob, let's give thanks for the gifts the office brings to you, and for the grace that will be channeled through you to the church.

The second reason we have for celebrating an ordination is a little darker. We light the candles and lay our hands on you because this gift is hard. It's one of God's gifts that could spell trouble, and we want to encourage you. The best form of encouragement is not advice or exhortation but blessing. Drew, we are determined not to let you go until we bless you.

Because it is hard, many if not most of these who have been called to ministry have tried to wriggle their way out of it. I am not talking about the usual puffery of false protestations. *Why me, Lord? What about the recording contract I was about to sign? Or the lucrative law practice I'm giving up?* The prophet Isaiah said, "I am an unclean man with unclean lips, and, frankly, I come from a people who don't deserve a ministry." I suppose one could say, with Jeremiah, "I am only a youth" (by the way, that argument has an unforgiving sell-by date). Or with Moses, "Who am I that I should go to Pharaoh?" and besides, "I am slow of speech and of tongue," to which God, who is growing weary with these excuses, replies, "Who has made man's mouth? I will be with your mouth." (And, incidentally, isn't it just like God to choose as his chief representative a person with a speech impediment?)

Drew, you must have sensed something of the darker side of ministry when you chose the Old Testament reading for tonight, the story of Jacob's wrestling with a mysterious stranger at the Jabbok Ford. This is not an ordination text. It's not an *ordinary* text. It doesn't contain a list of duties you must perform to please God or a congregation. Nor is it an inventory of personal traits needed to qualify for ordination. It goes deeper than that. It cuts to the basic questions. They are the preprofessional, postseminary questions that we all must ask and come to terms with: Who is God? How does God name me into the church? How will God use me during my time in this dangerous world?

You remember the story. Twenty years earlier Jacob had cheated his brother Esau out of his birthright. Esau was the elder twin. He deserved to receive the blessing. But the cunning Jacob went to his blind father, Isaac, dressed in animal fur to mimic his hunter brother (who, the King James Version says, "was an hairy man"). When Isaac asked, "Who are you?" the trickster lied, "I am Esau, dear father," with the result that he, and not his brother, received his blessing. Then he took off, married two wonderful women, and got rich. But he continued to be plagued by the nagging realization that he had duped his father, cheated his brother, and offended the God of his ancestors.

Fast-forward twenty years. The good news is that after a long absence Esau has sent word that he wants to meet his brother again. The bad news is that he is bringing four hundred men with him. Jacob is nervous. Four different times he says compulsively, "Oh, yes, I want to see Esau's face again" ("face" is the Hebrew equivalent of spending quality time with someone). He is afraid. He sends his wives, children, and cattle across the Jabbok ahead of him, but he settles down to sleep alone under the stars. In the night a "man"—a demigod? an angel?—assaults him. They wrestle all night, and when Jacob begins to get the better of this being, he asks for and receives a blessing. The stranger then touches the joint where the thigh connects to the hip and disables him. "Who are you?" Jacob asks. No answer. "Who are *you*?" the stranger asks. Twenty years after lying about his name, he tells the truth at last. "I am Jacob." "No," says the mysterious stranger, "you are Israel, and in you all the world shall be blessed." When the dawn comes, we see the trickster limping across the river to meet his brother. All he can say is, "I have seen God face-to-face and lived."

That morning, Jacob divides his family into two large groups, one to the left, one to the right, so that when Esau attacks him, at least half his family will escape. Then, in an uncharacteristic show of courage, Jacob walks out ahead of them to meet his brother. It's one of those special moments of truth in the Bible. It is high noon at the Jabbok. Esau rushes toward him and, instead of slitting his throat as expected, embraces him, and the two of them fall into one another's arms as if they had just won the World Series.

Jacob offers him gifts, which Esau sweetly refuses by saying, "I have enough, brother." Jacob replies, "Your face is like the face of God to me."

When God calls a person to ministry, peace does not descend upon the soul. No, that's when the struggle begins. Jacob becomes a symbol of Israel, a people that will always contend with God but will bear God's blessing to the world.

Tonight, only you, Drew, know the contours of your battlefield. Everyone's lines are drawn in different places. Some ministers instinctively sense that they can't possibly live up to the office to which they have been appointed. After all, we call it the "holy ministry," sometimes forgetting that it's the office and not the tenant that we're talking about. It's one thing when Jesus says to his disciples, "Be ye perfect, as your father in heaven is perfect." It's another altogether when the congregation says the same to its newly ordained pastor. As the apostle Paul, who had his share of problems, said, "Who is sufficient for these things?"

The call to ministry puts you where you don't always want to be, namely, in the public eye. It's one thing to hold a personal faith; it's another to be given the wisdom to exercise it on behalf of others. It's one thing to have holy words as a part of your passive, seminary vocabulary; it's another to speak them from the heart to someone who has come to the end of words.

Ministers labor under the myth of fluency. Isn't it obvious? Men and women become preachers because they are good with words and possess natural gifts for ministry. Unlike most of us, they are innately comfortable performing before large groups. But, Drew, as you have already discovered, writing a sermon is just another version of Wrestling with the Angel on Saturday night. Nowhere in the Bible do we meet a prophet or preacher who is having a hard time thinking of something to say. But for many of us, who in the course of our ministries will speak no fewer than three million words from the pulpit, knowing what to say can be a challenge.

The tradition offers scant comfort. Luther assures us, "Whom God wishes to heal, he first batters to pieces," or "God can draw a straight line with a crooked stick." For Jacob, it meant a hip displacement; for Ezekiel, exile; for Saint Paul, a temporary blinding followed by a permanent thorn in the flesh.

For Jesus, to whom God said, "You are my son; today I have begotten you," it meant a cross. For those who follow Jesus, this is *the* mark—*the* displacement par excellence. This is the credential you don't have to earn or achieve. At your baptism it was said, "Receive the sign of the cross, both upon the forehead and the breast, in token that you have been redeemed by Christ the crucified." That promise can never be taken from you, but it does leave an indelible mark.

Tonight, you are being ordered to the mark. It means that, like Jacob and Esau, you will be unwilling to live an unreconciled life. Instead, your ministry will constitute a countersign to the hatred and divisions that surround it.

Like Jacob, you will see the face of God in other faces, especially in those who suffer or who have been denied justice. You may be tempted to think that safety lies only in the company of those who bear the same mark, who speak the same language, and think as you do. A parish can be a sheltering institution, one that insulates the pastor from challenges that parishioners face on a daily basis. But that's not what ordination is all about.

With a city exploding in anger, CNN reported that one hundred pastors had spent the night walking the streets of Ferguson, Missouri. I'm guessing that few of them saw *that* coming on the night they were ordained. Like them, and like your namesake Jacob, you will find strength you didn't know you had.

Your ordination is a mere first step, and a very good one. You have refused to live an uncalled life. You have wrestled with this thing called vocation, and, like Jacob, you have said, "I will not let you go until you bless me."

Tonight, we bless you, Andrew Jacob Tucker—and we let you go. Courage!

ACKNOWLEDGMENTS

Permissions granted to reprint the following:

"God Has Gone Up with a Shout." In *Exploring and Proclaiming the Apostles' Creed*. Edited by Roger E. Van Harn. Grand Rapids: Eerdmans, 2004.

The following sermons were first published in *Faith & Leadership*, Duke Divinity School: "The View from the Ditch" (February 2011); "That's When the Trouble Starts" (February 2017). http://www.faithandleadership.com/.

The following sermons were first published in *The Christian Century*: "Acknowledgment" (vol. 116, no. 7 [March 3, 1999]: 245); "The Shape of Ashes" (vol. 132, no. 4 [February 18, 2015]: 10–11); "Stripped Bare" (vol. 129, no. 6 [March 21, 2012]: 11–12); "Odd Job: The Secret Gift of Ministry" (vol. 121, no. 7 [April 6, 2004]: 24–25); "A Sense of Ending" (vol. 116, no. 8 [March 10, 1999]: 277); "Waiting for Good News: Holy Saturday in a Time of Plague" (vol. 137, no. 8 [April 8, 2020]: 12–13).

"I Have Seen the Future." In *Sermons from Duke Chapel: Voices from "A Great and Towering Church."* Durham, NC: Duke University Press, 2005.

"The River. In Memory of Flannery O'Connor" and "The Heart of a Heartless World." In *The Minister's Manual 2006*. Edited by James W. Cox. San Francisco: Jossey-Bass, 2005.